The

Toddler's Busy Play Book

Over 500 Creative Games, Activities, Crafts and Recipes for Your Very Busy Toddler

Robin McClure

 SOURCEBOOKS, INC.®
NAPERVILLE, ILLINOIS

PLAYSKOOL and BUSY are trademarks of Hasbro and are used with permission.
© 2007 Hasbro. All Rights Reserved.

Copyright © 2007 by Sourcebooks, Inc.
Cover and internal design © 2007 by Sourcebooks, Inc.
Cover photo © Punchstock

PLAYSKOOL and BUSY are trademarks of Hasbro and are used with permission. © 2007 Hasbro. All Rights Reserved.
Sourcebooks and the colophon are registered trademarks of Sourcebooks, Inc.

All rights reserved. No part of this book may be reproduced in any form or by any electronic or mechanical means including information storage and retrieval systems—except in the case of brief quotations embodied in critical articles or reviews—without permission in writing from its publisher, Sourcebooks, Inc.

This publication is designed to provide accurate and authoritative information in regard to the subject matter covered. It is sold with the understanding that nether the publisher nor Hasbro are engaged in rendering legal, accounting, or other professional service. If legal advice or other expert assistance is required, the services of a competent professional person should be sought.—*From a Declaration of Principles Jointly Adopted by a Committee of the American Bar Association and a Committee of Publishers and Associations*

All activities within this book are to be conducted with appropriate adult supervision. Care must be taken by parents, guardians, and caregivers to select activities that are appropriate for the age of the children. The authors, the publisher, and Hasbro shall have neither liability nor responsibility to any person or entity with respect to any mishaps or damage caused, or alleged to be caused, directly or indirectly by the information contained in this book.

All brand names and product names used in this book are trademarks, registered trademarks, or trade names of their respective holders. Sourcebooks, Inc., is not associated with any product or vendor in this book.

Play-Doh® is a registered trademark of Hasbro. All Rights Reserved.

Published by Sourcebooks, Inc.
P.O. Box 4410, Naperville, Illinois 60567-4410
(630) 961-3900
Fax: (630) 961-2168
www.sourcebooks.com

Library of Congress Cataloging-in-Publication Data

McClure, Robin.
 The Playskool toddler's busy play book : 500 activities for any situation - sick days, play dates, holiday cheer, indoors, outdoors, and educational play / Robin McClure.
    p. cm.
 Includes index.
 ISBN-13: 978-1-4022-0933-8
 ISBN-10: 1-4022-0933-9
 1. Toddlers–Development. 2. Child development. 3. Early childhood education–Activity programs. 4. Creative activities and seat work. 5. Play. 6. Parent and child. I. Title.

HQ774.5.M393 2007
649'.5–dc22

                    2007009581

Printed and bound in the United States of America.
BG 10 9 8 7 6 5 4 3 2

Contents

A Word about Cleanup and Safety

The activities and projects in this book are intended to be easy, low- or no-cost things you and your toddler (and your toddler's siblings or playmates) can do together. Many use only your imagination, but where materials are recommended, most are things you probably have around the house or are easily procured.

We do recommend you customize each of these activities to your child. For example, use extra caution with all edible projects, particularly with children with allergies or potential for allergies. With kids at toddler age, some allergies may still be undiscovered, so we ask that you closely monitor your child's use of all materials.

Any project requiring hot or cold materials (such as hot water or ice, or items that are baked, such as cookies) should be handled only by adults until it is safe for the child to touch. Children should only use safety scissors if appropriate and only then under an adult's watchful eye. Keep small materials away from infants and, where appropriate, from toddlers too. Materials such as paint, markers, food coloring, glue, etc., should always be tested first to ensure they don't leave permanent marks on tables, floors, walls, etc., and especially to ensure that they're washable off skin and clothing. If you're not sure, skip the activity—there are hundreds more in this book that will prove loads of fun!

Acknowledgments

There is no roadmap when it comes to toddlers; just like snowflakes, no two youngsters are alike in their play preferences, personalities, skills, or interests. So it is with special admiration and appreciation that I thank my children's past and present care providers and early education teachers for their wisdom and distinctive ideas for this book, along with the friends who enthusiastically provided me with their own cherished toddler activities. (Angele, Cheryl, Emily, Gina, Kim, Leslie, Megan, Teena, Teresa, Theresa, Tracey, and Verone—you're the best!). I'd also like to acknowledge contributions from my peers at Grapevine-Colleyville and Birdville school districts, who selflessly dedicate their lives to working with children every day. A special thanks is extended to my sister-in-law Susan Watkins, who is not only an amazing mom, but a dedicated public school teacher as well. Huge hugs go to my husband,

Rick, and to our children, Hunter, Erin, and Connor, who demonstrated tremendous patience, love, and support throughout my first book-writing venture. Finally I want to acknowledge my cherished parents, Bonnie and Rod Watkins, and my husband's family, Dan and Dorothy McClure, for setting positive examples of how to raise toddlers the right way through lots of love and parental involvement, and who survived to tell about it!

Introduction

"I'm bored!" Perhaps no other two words can so quickly evoke a reaction from parents and caregivers alike than these when uttered from the lips of a toddler. This inevitable complaint can occur anywhere, at any time, and it may follow a full day of fun at a park, a week-long family vacation, or even an enthralling adventure. A constant need for activity and stimulation, after all, defines the life of the ever-busy, constantly curious, and always-on-the go toddler. Our job as adults, after making sure kids in our care stay safe and healthy, is to keep up with them and to nourish their mental and physical growth!

Caring for toddlers may be the most extraordinary and exasperating experience you'll ever encounter. Toddlers are often thrill-seekers by nature; they are utterly captivated by stimulating events, and they thrive on exploring every aspect of their blossoming world. They are often fearless, without a care about consequences or danger. Adding to the complexity of raising kids of this age is the fact that no two youngsters are the same, so what piques the fascination of one may prove totally uninteresting to another.

Parents are often astounded to find that, despite being siblings, their children have distinct interests, desires, and fascinations. This means that every time a new child enters your world, you will most likely need an entirely new game plan. I learned this fact firsthand by raising my own brood of three.

My oldest son, Hunter, never liked structured coloring or anything with wheels (ruling out cars, trucks, and airplanes). He was, however, utterly crazy about pirates and ships, so his early childhood was filled with adventures on the high seas and costumes that befitted a captain.

My daughter, Erin, revels in stuffed animals and all things "girlish." Her room is decorated in hot pink and zebra stripes, and it holds an extensive collection of dolls and CDs for dance parties and pretend productions, yet she dismisses most costumes and creative wear as "itchy." She is always on the lookout for that next big thrill.

My youngest son, Connor, is the shy one of the bunch. He is more hesitant to try new things. He colors beautifully within the lines, but he stresses when asked to create something on a blank sheet of paper. He is just shy of being obsessed with cars, trucks, trains, planes, boats, robots, gadgets, and anything that makes noise. (My husband, Rick, a former miniature car collector, just loves this about him!)

On the surface, my kids have very little in common; each is extraordinary and quite precious in her or his own way. Their differences just mean that I've gone through a lot of different toys, activities, dress-up pieces, and books through the years!

For parents, raising toddlers can mean the chance to relive the preciousness of childhood, but these magical memories will happen only if you slow down and allow your youngsters to lead you back in time. A walk around the block can take an exasperatingly long time with a little one who wants to stop and look, touch, smell, listen, and perhaps even taste all that surrounds him—but therein lies the true charm.

If your daughter or son wants to step (or not) on every sidewalk crack, examine a blade of grass, pick up a bug, or just twirl in a gust of wind, you should encourage her or him. And what's stopping you from joining in as well? These experiences are what help our kids learn and grow. Every chance to jump in mud puddles, sing in the rain, or watch the sunset together before bedtime is a moment that may come, pass quickly, and be gone forever.

Isn't it sad how we always rush kids through these moments because we've become such clock watchers? Have you ever seen a youngster playing alone or not getting a chance to ask about something because a parent or caregiver is too busy yakking on a cell phone or mindlessly watching TV?

Has this ever happened to you? I recently took my brood out for some good ole mom-kid time, and then sadly watched a man shoo his son to "go play" while dad remained engrossed with reading and writing text messages and taking work calls. It was another missed opportunity to learn all about life's enchantments through the eyes of a youngster, one moment and one miracle at a time.

I find myself becoming the "tsk-tsk" type of mom, scolding my kids for some of their less-than-ideal behaviors, when in reality they aren't (usually) trying to get a rise out of me, but are just vying for my attention or reveling in something new they've learned.

My daughter taught my youngest son how to burp one lazy afternoon, a skill he now likes to show off with great pride and absolute gusto. He makes an annoying screech when racing his small cars down an imaginary highway, and my daughter cranks the music too loud for my mature ears.

I've written this book with the hope that it will help you bring your focus back to staying involved with your kids.

But my inner voice urges me to remain calm and to engage. After all, when was the last time I challenged my son to a toy car race or showed my daughter one of my own crazed dance moves?

Sadly, I don't play with my kids often enough because I find myself burdened with my own adult world and its overwhelming responsibilities. (Anyone else struggling with this?) I've written this book with the hope that it will help you bring your focus back to staying involved with your kids. It is full of activities that will guarantee a good time and put a smile on any toddler's face—and on yours as well!

> My most sincere wish is that at least one of these 500 activities (and hopefully many, many more) will reconnect you with the child in your care in a truly touching and memorable way.

The Playskool Toddler's Busy Play Book offers an array of activities, crafts, recipes, and fun family adventures that are neither costly nor difficult—and that are perfect for preschoolers! Some activities require nothing more than imagination and interaction. Others require simple craft materials, many of which can be found around the home. And in honor of the uniqueness of each of our very precious children, there is a wide assortment of activities—500 in all—that will provide countless hours of learning, interaction, adventure, play, and family fun.

Any one of the ideas in this book can provide the perfect bonding time between parent and child, between grandparent and grandchild, or even between a babysitter and her young charge. Some activities you've undoubtedly heard of or participated in with your child or during your own childhood. Others may result in a new family tradition or become holiday favorites that can be shared year after year. Perhaps some activities will spark an original idea for you to try with your own family. My most sincere wish is that at least one of these 500 activities (and hopefully many, many more) will reconnect you with the child in your care in a truly touching and memorable way.

May you be blessed with busy hands, loving hearts, and lots of memories in the making!

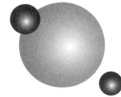

Seasonal Celebrations

Every season brings a reason to celebrate with plentiful food, fun, and fantasies inspired by Mother Nature.

Winter

Colorful Coffee Filter Snowflakes

Whoever said snowflakes have to be white? Add some color to Ole Man Winter with some bright and cheery kid-crafted snowflakes that will brighten up any room or mood!

Materials

- large flat-bottom coffee filters
- markers
- kid-friendly scissors
- paper towels
- water
- stickers or glitter, if desired

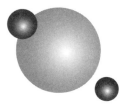

Place a coffee filter flat on a surface (spread newspaper or other paper underneath the filter to avoid any mess), and have your toddler color the surface of the coffee filter with bright markers in any design; it won't matter whether it's scribbled on or solidly colored. When your child has finished, fold the filter into fourths and have your kid create some simple snowflake designs by cutting into the pattern (adult guidance is needed here!). After simple cuts have been made, reopen the filter to its original size and then wet it down (preferably using the sprayer from the kitchen sink or water from a water bottle). This makes the colors blend and run together, creating a tie-dye effect! If desired, further decorate the snowflake with stickers or glitter. Make several and hang them around the child's room using paperclips or string.

Edible Snowflakes

Your kids will beg to make these snowflakes as a tasty winter treat!

Ingredients
- large flour tortillas
- butter
- cinnamon sugar

Fold flour tortillas into fourths and then let kids cut them as they would cut out paper snowflakes. (Adults should cut shapes for small kids.) Open them out full-size, place them on a plate, and then let kids spread them with butter and sprinkle them with cinnamon sugar. (Make sure the butter is soft enough to spread easily without tearing the tortilla.)

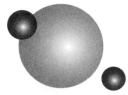

Finger Paint Pudding

Looking for something to do on a cold or rainy day? How about drawing with edible finger paint?

Ingredients

- 1 small package of instant pudding in the flavor of your choice (or consider making a large batch of vanilla pudding, dividing it into several bowls, and then adding food coloring to create some fun color choices)

Prepare the pudding according to the directions on the box. Let the pudding set until thick. Get kids to finger-paint with pudding on a clean cookie sheet. They can lick and paint at the same time. Let them use a spatula or other cooking tool to make interesting shapes and patterns as part of their tasty creation.

Graham Cracker Snow Cabins

Have your child construct a simple cabin out of graham crackers and peanut butter (or marshmallow whip for those children with peanut allergies), using a Styrofoam or paper plate as the base. Use canned white icing to form snow on the rooftop and around the base. If desired, accessorize the simple cabin with miniature chocolate chips or other candy.

Hot Chocolate Chef

Even very young kids will feel like chefs when they are making their very own hot chocolate. Show them how to make the homemade variety, either by heating milk over the stove and adding in cocoa and sugar, or by just opening an individual serving size of hot cocoa mix, pouring it into a cup, and adding hot water. (Parents: only you should heat and handle the hot water or milk! Your child can add the cocoa or mix.) Let your youngster have his very own special mug or cup to use for drinking hot chocolate on those cold winter days. Sit and enjoy together.

Marshmallow Snowman

Not every child gets the opportunity to build a traditional snowman. But, snowfall or not, parents can help build a marshmallow snowman that is a fun and tasty treat!

Materials

- large marshmallows
- red and black licorice strings (or similar string candy)
- raisins, mini M&Ms, or other small candies
- mini carrots (cut into slivers)
- whipped cream (from a spray can or tub)
- small plate
- toothpicks
- small marshmallows
- whatever else sparks your imagination!

Start by putting whipped cream on the plate to represent snow; this will become the snowman's base. Use a toothpick to connect two large marshmallows, one on top of the other. Now comes the fun part! Trim licorice strings to create a scarf, buttons, or whatever your child would like. Next, place a small marshmallow on top (using a toothpick) to make a hat; do the same for arms. Use M&Ms, Skittles, or other ingredients to represent other snowman parts and accessories. Use a sliver of a small carrot for the nose. And, finally, the best part: After building the perfect snowman, kids get to eat it! (Be sure to remove the toothpicks first.)

Mini Bells

Make jingle bells using small paper cups.

Materials
- Dixie cups or other small paper cups used with dispensers
- jingle bells
- chenille stems (pipe cleaners)
- glitter glue
- markers

Poke two holes in the base of each upside-down cup. Fold the chenille stems in half and place each end through a hole, leaving a small loop at the top. Twist the chenille stem to hold it in place. Attach a jingle bell to each end of the stem inside the cup and then twist into place. Let your toddler adorn the bells with glitter glue, markers, or any other decorative item, as desired.

Mitten Match

Cut some simple mitten shapes out of paper and then create unique designs on each pair. Shuffle them together and have your toddler match each mitten to its mate.

S'more Snack

Your toddler can make this treat all by herself and share it with the rest of the family! It's a simple snack, perfect to munch on while cuddling next to a warm fireplace.

Ingredients

- 1 box of honey graham cereal
- 1 bag of semisweet chocolate chips
- 1 bag of mini marshmallows

Combine ingredients and serve in small paper cups. Store in an airtight container.

Snowflake Fantasy

Have your toddler pretend she is a snowflake. How does she fall from the sky, and what does she become? Will she make a big pile of snow? Become part of a snowman? Turn into snow ice cream? Ask for ideas about what a single snowflake can become.

Sock Snowman

Create a silly sock snowman to celebrate winter.

Materials
- large men's tube sock
- single roll of toilet paper (intact)
- medium Styrofoam ball
- large pipe cleaner (orange)
- large google eyes
- large pom-pom (any color)
- several small pom-poms (black)
- rubber band
- craft glue
- three buttons

Place the toilet paper roll inside the sock and push it all the way down to the bottom. Next, place the Styrofoam ball on top of the toilet paper roll inside the sock. Twist the rubber band on top to close the sock and create a winter hat. To decorate, glue the eyes in place, then cut off a small piece of orange pipe cleaner, bend it in half, and push it through the sock into the Styrofoam for a "carrot" nose. Glue small black pom-poms into a "coal" smile shape, and then glue the large pom-pom to the tip of the sock (for the end of the hat). Finally, glue buttons onto the toilet paper portion of the sock.

Winter Placemat

Create a winter placemat using a large foam sheet as a base (for easy wiping off) and have your young artist create a scene with designs such as snowflakes, snowmen, and anything else that denotes the season, using different-colored foam sheets. Help with cutting out shapes (craft stores often have precut foam winter shapes as well), and then have your toddler glue them in place using a glue stick. For younger toddlers, use the stick-on foam shapes (simply peel off the adhesive back). Add some extra sparkle using glitter glue!

Winter What-If Game

Turn the winter season into a game of "what if." Pose some weather-related questions to your toddler to start some interesting conversations. Consider asking, "What if it turns really cold tonight, and it rains. What would come out of the sky? What's the difference between rain and sleet? What if it snows? What will we do together?"

Spring

Bean Plant Sprout

Youngsters today don't often get to experience the sprouting of a plant from seed. That can be easily remedied with the simple project of having young children plant a lima bean (or something similar, such as a corn kernel) using dirt or potting soil in a small paper cup. Even very young kids enjoy watering a plant (use a tablespoon or something similar that won't result in accidental overwatering) and then watching the plant sprout and grow with water and sunlight. Older toddlers who show interest in a bean plant might also find growing a simple tomato plant fascinating, especially when they get to eat the result!

Butterfly Garden

What child doesn't like digging in the dirt, planting flowers, and admiring fluttery friends who might come for a visit? Depending on where you live, butterflies may be in abundance during much of the year. Creating a colorful landscape will add even more delight to the butterfly watching.

First choose a sunny location that is sheltered from wind. Find a couple of flat stones; dark-colored, smooth ones that retain heat are preferable because butterflies love to sun themselves after a meal. Insects require water, so make a small butterfly pond in the mud. Or improvise and use a lid from plasticware or from a household item such as a butter tub.

Finally, choose blooming plants. Find a hearty plant that loves the sun. In the South, lantana makes a great choice; other great options are hydrangeas, cornflowers, geraniums, scabiosa, and the plant aptly called the "butterfly bush." You'll also want to provide food for larvae. Consider Mexican milkweed or passion vine. If feasible, take your toddler with you to the nursery and let her help you select a few plants (only a small space is needed).

Include in your design a place to sit in the garden, such as a bench, chairs, or sitting stones. Soon you'll be ready for some spectacular butterfly watching as well as having a quiet place to read with your toddler and soak in the sun!

Crepe Paper Wind Sock

Celebrate spring and its windy roar with a handcrafted wind sock. These wind socks can also be made to reflect a theme or holiday.

Materials

- foam paper (preferred for durability), construction paper, or plain white paper
- hole puncher (or scissors)
- stapler or tape
- crepe paper
- materials for decorating (markers, foam shapes, glitter glue, stickers, odds and ends)
- yarn or string

Have your child decorate one side of a thin foam sheet using markers, glitter glue, stickers, foam shapes, or any odds and ends. With adult help, shapes can be cut out of the foam and then glued on as accent pieces. Once that is finished, roll the foam sheet lengthwise into a cylinder and staple it to hold its shape. Staple or tape strips of crepe paper at one end. Punch four holes at equal distances apart near the top edge, tie a piece of yarn to each end, and join the pieces of yarn in the middle with a knot. (This will serve as the handle.) Toddlers may like to run around outside with the wind sock to watch the tails (crepe paper) soar, and then find a place to hang it where they can watch it move in the wind.

Duck Watch

Take your toddler to a local duck pond to visit with the ducks and see the new ducklings. Animal farms, feed stores, and pet shops often have ducklings in the spring, so these are great options for duck watching as well.

Egg Yolk Paint

Let your toddlers decorate cookies with egg yolk paint. Help your toddler crack an egg and separate the yolk from the white. Add ½ teaspoon of water to the yolk and mix. Add food coloring. Shape sugar cookie dough into an egg or other spring design and let your toddler paint on the dough with the colored yolk. Bake according to sugar cookie directions; the egg yolk paint will bake the design right into the cookie!

Flower Fun

Create colorful flower petals out of paper and let your child have fun playing a safer version of Pin the Tail on the Donkey. Apply rolled tape or double-sided tape to the backs of the petals and have your blindfolded toddler stick them onto a large drawing of a flower stem. You can add some leaves to make the outcome even funnier!

Galloping Foal

Have your child act like a young foal out to enjoy the spring sunshine. Gallop across the backyard, whinny into the wind, and kick your legs out in sheer enjoyment of the beautiful weather.

Mud Puddle Hurdle

Turn the next rainy spring day into a mud puddle–hurdling event! Don some rain boots and see who can jump the farthest over a puddle. Who can make the biggest splash? Toddlers love stepping in mud puddles, and, on occasion, you should let go and cater to those whims. Maybe even join in!

Rain Gauge

There are fancier ways to make a rain gauge, but for toddlers, just use a glass jar that you mark measurements on using a ruler and a permanent marker. Place the jar outside where it won't tip over and let your youngster check on it to see how much it rains. As an educational exercise, you can ask comparison questions such as whether today's rainfall is "less or more" than the last time you checked.

Spring Flowers

These tissue flowers provide a cheery welcome to springtime.

Materials
- 3–5 different colored sheets of tissue paper
- pipe cleaners
- vase (if desired)

Let your child choose three or four different colored sheets of tissue paper and set them on top of each other. Show how to fold the paper into an accordion fold (or fanfold) and wrap a pipe cleaner or twist tie in the middle of the folded tissue. Next, have your toddler carefully open his flower by pulling the different colors of paper either up or down as desired to separate and "fluff." Add a pipe cleaner stem. If you like, you can even craft leaves from additional pipe cleaners.

Umbrella Dance

Get out your umbrellas and perform an impromptu umbrella dance during the next light spring rain. Twirl your umbrellas, dance in circles, and just enjoy an improvised moment of fun!

Summer

Bob for Blueberries

You've heard of bobbing for apples, but your toddler will love bobbing for blueberries instead! Place the fruit in some water and let him eat whatever he can catch with his tongue.

Flip-Flop Fun

For fashionable summer fun, you and your child can make a unique pair of flip-flops for a caregiver, babysitter, or friend. Have your youngster help you pick out some ribbon and gemstones or other decorative items to add to a pair of flip-flops. Cut a 19-inch strip of ribbon (you can always trim the ends shorter, depending on the style and size of flip-flop selected) and fashion a pretty bow from it. Trim the ends off at a diagonal. Use a hot-melt glue gun to fasten the ribbon onto the Y-part of the flip-flop (adults need to do this part, please). Add a charm, stone, or other item to the center of the bow (not using anything is okay too). Your toddler will get a kick out of making them, and will love giving them as a gift even more.

Ice Cream in a Bag

Who needs to wait for hand-cranked homemade ice cream when kids can create their own individual, serving–size creation in no time and with no mess! This homemade ice cream recipe uses a toddler's energy for a delicious outcome!

Ingredients

- 1 cup milk (use chocolate milk if preferred)
- 2 tsp. sugar
- ½ tsp. vanilla extract
- 1-quart resealable bag
- 1-gallon resealable bag
- several spoonfuls of rock salt
- enough ice to cover the small bag

Place milk, sugar, and vanilla into the small bag and zip the bag securely. Put the small bag into the larger bag. Add ice and salt. Let your toddler shake the bag gently for about 5 minutes. When it is done, the ice cream will have the consistency of soft serve. Enjoy!

Made in the Shade

Establish a shady outdoor area for special summer reading. Grab some chairs or a blanket and establish this as your special reading area. Find books about summer that involve outdoor activities, vacations, or just ways to soak up the sunshine and read them with your child.

Painting Van Goghs

It's summertime, so why not let your little artists showcase their talent outdoors? Set up a large sheet of paper (or even use the large roll-sheets found at craft supply and teacher supply stores) either on an easel or on a flat surface. Dress your toddler in a swimsuit or old clothes, provide selections of water-based paint, and let the art begin! To encourage artistic expression, look at some simple art books together beforehand.

Rain Sticks

If a summer drought is affecting your area, help your toddler make a rain stick to summon the rain.

Materials
- paper towel rolls
- noisemakers such as rice, beans, small pebbles, or even marbles
- cardboard cut to fit ends
- construction paper in colors of your choice
- scissors
- tape
- decorations as desired

Cut a circle out of cardboard or poster board to fit one end of the paper towel roll, and tape it securely shut. Have your toddler drop items into the tube. While covering the open end with your hand, turn the rain stick from end to end to find out how it sounds. Let kids experiment with adding more or using less of the filling until it sounds just right. Use another cardboard circle to close the other end of the tube. You can tape construction paper over the roll to make it more attractive, and then let your child decorate it.

Splash Tag

Play a friendly game of splash tag! Dress your toddler in a swimsuit and step outdoors. The players run from the person who is "it," who tries to tag people out by throwing a wet sponge. If tagged, that person becomes "it." For a larger group of kids, give everyone a sponge and keep a bucket of water nearby for replenishing.

Tepee Hideout

Build your toddler a simple tepee for hours of backyard fun.

Materials
- 3 white PVC pipes (8-foot pipes work best)
- rope
- canvas tarp, cloth, or blanket

Using the rope, tie the PVC pipes together about 20–24 inches from the tops and then stand them up like a tripod. If possible, dig out an area of the ground so that the pipes are planted firmly. Cover the tepee frame with tarp, cloth, blanket, or whatever you have available.

Watermelon Cookies

Cut a seedless watermelon into ½-inch slices. Place the slices on a flat surface outdoors (to avoid a mess in your house) and use cookie cutters to cut out fun shapes. Kids will love eating their tasty "cookies," and the shapes make the fruit easier to handle!

Worm Dirt

This is a favorite recipe with toddlers, and it makes a great summer dessert. For a special flair, serve the treat in a plastic bag or plastic wrap placed inside a small clay pot (so that it's clean and leak-proof).

Ingredients
- instant chocolate pudding
- milk
- Oreo (or other chocolate) cookies
- whipped topping
- snack-size plastic bags
- gummy worms

Make and refrigerate the instant chocolate pudding with youngsters. Then have them separate the Oreo cookies and scrape off the cream with a small spatula, spoon, or dull knife and put the cookies in one pile and the cream filling in another pile. (For an easier recipe, forgo the cookie separation and just let toddlers crumble entire cookies in the bag.) Put the cookies into a plastic bag. Then close the bag and have the kids break them up into "dirt" by squeezing the bag. Pour the crumbled dirt into the bottom of a cup or small clay pot lined with plastic wrap. Leave just a little bit in the bag for topping, if desired. Next, scoop chocolate pudding into each cup. Place a scoop of whipped topping on the top of each cup and add the white cream filling to it, as desired. Sprinkle the remaining crumbled chocolate cookie topping and then garnish with a couple of gummy worms. Enjoy!

Autumn Leaves

Cut a piece of brown foam paper into a basic tree design with some branches and let your youngsters decorate their own fall tree.

Materials
- 1 sheet of brown foam paper
- 1 sheet of blue foam paper
- assorted colors of foam paper to be cut into fall-colored leaves
- glue stick

Have your toddler glue the tree base onto the blue paper. Cut leaf shapes (keep it simple by cutting simple oval shapes, if desired) while your toddler is gluing on the trunk. Then let your youngster glue leaves onto the tree. Show how some can be glued around the base or in the area to denote fallen and falling leaves. This makes a great autumn craft decoration.

Edible Apple Prints

Who would have thought kids could have so much fun with a craft that they can eat?

Materials/Ingredients
- apples
- yogurt (either buy kinds that already have a color or add in a few drops of food coloring)
- paper plates

Slice apples in different ways to create some interesting shapes. Pour a few different types of yogurt onto a plate and then give your child a paper plate to create his masterpiece. Show him how to dip apples into yogurt and then create prints on the paper plate to create edible art. He can eat the project each step of the way and create some fun apple prints too!

Fall Journal

Create a fall journal of fun things to do this season with magazine and newspaper cutouts, illustrations, stamps, and more. Have your youngster include anything that is reminiscent of the season—for example, brightly colored leaves, cooler temperatures, and fall sports such as football and soccer. Include blank pages so that things can be added throughout the season. Make a separate journal for each season!

Falling Leaves Game

Have your youngster pretend she is a leaf on a tree, soaking up the sunshine. Then imagine the wind blowing and the leaf falling. What will the leaf do in the wind before eventually landing on the ground?

Food Harvest Drive

Have your toddler help you to conduct a food harvest drive. With the support of friends, neighbors, or caregivers, initiate a food drive over a few weeks. Each week can feature a different staple: canned vegetables, pasta, peanut butter, dinner mixes, etc. (If possible, call your local food bank and see what supplies are most needed.) You and your toddler can design a simple flyer that your child can pass out to participants. Some food banks will arrange for pick ups; otherwise, you can have your child accompany you when delivering food items.

Leaf Rubbings

Young kids are utterly amazed at all the neat shapes that can be found outdoors. In the fall take a nature hike at a local park or around your neighborhood. Have your child collect leaves of various shapes and sizes. Once inside, take a piece of plain white paper and place it over a leaf. Next, have your child color over it. The image of the leaf will appear on the paper. Encourage the use of different colors for various leaf shapes to make a more interesting collection. If your child is old enough, have him cut around the image (adults will need to do this for very young children). Provide a simple storage basket for the rubbings for your child to keep and return to often.

Moon Festival

Fall is a perfect time to celebrate the moon. From the harvest moon (so named, according to legend, because it shines brightly enough for farmers to continue their harvest work through the evening) to autumn moon celebrations (because the moon appears larger during this season), kids will love learning about the moon and its lore. Have a moon walk, in which you walk in the dark to gaze at the moon. Have a backyard moon dance, or even act like coyotes and howl at the full moon!

Nut Adventure

Gather some nuts and let your toddler act like a squirrel. (You can also buy nuts or use other items as pretend nuts.) What do squirrels do when they find a nut? How do they prepare for the winter season ahead? Make it a game by hiding 10 nuts and then letting your youngster find them. Let your child create a squirrel burrow and swish his imaginary bushy tail.

Pumpkin Family

You and your toddler can use mini pumpkins to make a pumpkin family as a festive fall decoration. Use curled pipe cleaners to create hair (an adult may need to poke holes for the pipe cleaners using a skewer or similar object) and make the hairdo as simple or as zany as you want. Add a face with markers and, with heavy paper, craft small place cards that depict the family members' names or nicknames.

Seasonal Word Tricks

Have fun with your toddler by talking about how the season names spring and fall can also mean something different. Ask her what the different meanings are for these seasonal names. Can your youngster fall this fall? Can she spring around the room in the springtime? What other words have more than one meaning?

Squirrel Mix

Mix up a fall treat with cereal, nuts, cranberries, mini marshmallows, and even chocolate chips. Enjoy it at the park on a beautiful autumn day.

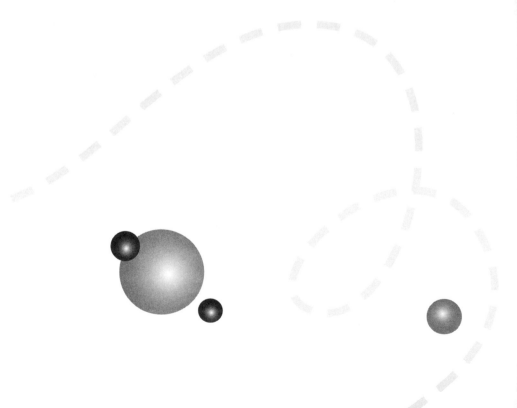

2

Holiday Fun

Ever-fascinated toddlers,
marveling at decorations
and squealing with anticipation
over every activity and
observance, are a delight to
share the holidays with.

New Year's Day

Annual Time Capsule

Create a family time capsule for the year. A cylindrical snack canister works well. Have each member of the family write down or state goals for the coming year and successes (and even regrets) from the previous year. Young toddlers may need help to recall events or milestones, but may be particularly proud of learning to swim or regretful of falling off the monkey bars and hurting an arm, for example. Throughout the year tuck in notes of special achievements or highlights. On the next New Year's Day open and review the time capsule together. Tuck in any additional summaries from the year and be sure to include a photograph or two of everyone. Close it up and then begin a new time capsule for the new year. These will surely become some of your most treasured keepsakes!

Family Goals

Have each family member set three goals for the upcoming year. The first should reflect something they would like to continue or improve on from the previous year. The second should be something new that they would like to try. The third should be family related. Adults can help toddlers think about these concepts by providing some suggestions. ("Didn't you say you wanted to try T-ball next year?") Post the goals of each family member in a place where they can be seen and remembered. The following December, have the family review the goals, talk about accomplishments and joys, and then think about the goals they want to set for next year!

New Year Crackers (Treat Tubes)

Fill empty paper towel roll tubes with small goodies and wrap them up for a New Year's treat.

Materials

- paper towel roll tubes
- gift wrap or tissue paper
- small treats (candy or inexpensive toys or goody items)
- tape
- ribbon

Fill tubes with goodies of your choice, stuff them with tissue to fill the remaining space, and then wrap the tubes and tie both ends with ribbon. Tape the paper down to prevent any peeking. On New Year's eve or New Year's morning, let your toddler enjoy a special New Year's surprise. This also works well for Fourth of July fun.

New Year's Day Traditions

Make New Year's Day a family day by initiating some silly traditions that you can carry forward each year. Ideas include staying in pajamas all day, eating breakfast for dinner and vice versa, or baking a birthday cake to celebrate Baby New Year. Let your toddler have a hand in planning some family fun!

Martin Luther King Jr.'s Birthday

Dream Share

Martin Luther King Jr. is known for his famous "I have a dream" speech, so why not celebrate his birthday by asking family members to share their dreams for the future? Have your kids draw a picture of their dream or, over a special family meal, talk about what they'd like to become when they grow up. Use this holiday, celebrated in the United States on the third Monday in January, as a time to discuss your child's dreams. Be sure to share your own too!

Groundhog Day

Shadow or No Shadow Survey

Groundhog Day is celebrated every year on February 2, and according to tradition, on this day a special groundhog named Punxsutawney Phil leaves the burrow where he has been hibernating to discover whether the cold winter weather will continue. If Punxsutawney Phil sees his shadow, it means six more weeks of winter. If he does not see his shadow, it means spring is just around the corner. Have your toddler guess whether the groundhog will see his shadow, and poll the rest of the family too; then report the results. Take advantage of this unique holiday to show your youngster a photo of a groundhog and talk about its habitat.

Valentine's Day

Book of Love

Cut 10 identically sized heart shapes out of plain white paper (a 5-inch by 4-inch size works well). Then cut two identical heart shapes using white or red construction paper. Stack the plain white paper hearts, and then place one colored heart on top of the stack and one on the bottom; staple them all together in a corner to create a small book. Have your toddler think of 10 things he loves and on each page draw a picture or find a sticker that conveys the message. This same idea can be used for a Valentine's Day gift, with the child expressing 10 things he likes about a person (teacher, parent, grandparent, etc.). Attach a small candy or treat to the front to complete the touching holiday sentiment!

I Love You Contest

Have a contest about how much you love each other and see who can create the biggest love whopper! Example: "I love you all the way to the sun and back." Or "I love you all the way to the very deepest part of the biggest ocean and back." Make it a lovefest and always end the game with a big hug!

Lovin' Bookmark

For Valentine's Day have your toddler create some very special bookmarks that show a loving appeal.

Materials
- foam paper in Valentine's Day colors
- glue
- markers
- scissors
- photos of your child
- optional decorations (foam hearts, sequins, stickers, etc.) as desired

Cut a 7-inch by 1½-inch rectangle of foam paper. This will form the base part of the bookmark. Cut out a large foam-paper heart (about 3½-inch wide is ideal). Trim a photo of your child into a heart shape the same size as the foam-paper heart. Have your child assemble the bookmark by gluing the heart to the base and then her photo to the heart. Let her decorate as desired. On the base, write a Valentine's Day message and include the child's name.

Reading Keepsake

Every year around Valentine's Day, videotape your child reading the beloved children's book *Guess How Much I Love You* with someone special. Record while your child and that special person talk about how much they love each other and why. As your child grows, he will be able to read the book with someone and then by himself, all of which you should continue to record. By the time your child is grown, you will have a priceless collection of memories and loving conversations.

Reasons Why I Love You

Establish a loving tradition by providing your toddler with a "Top 10 List of Reasons You Are Loved." Include silly reasons, poignant memories, and notable successes! Read it aloud on Valentine's Day. Be sure to date it, and keep it in a special place for safekeeping. Each year, read the new top 10 list together, and then look at previous years' lists too.

Silly Love Song

Create a silly love song for you to sing to your youngster on Valentine's Day. Croon it to her as a wake-up call, and then encourage your toddler to create one especially for you! Simple rhyming words and patterns make it easy. Sentimental parents should write down the lyrics to make a tender keepsake!

President's Day

Coins and Bills

Use this holiday to show your child various U.S. coins and bills bearing pictures of past presidents. Talk to them about who these men were and why they are an important part of our country's history. Have kids sort and stack the coins and bills.

President for a Day

If your child could be President of the United States for a day, what would she do? Ask your toddler to think of actions she would take, what she would eat, and where she would live. Does your youngster know what a president is? Why do we have one, and how does a person get chosen for this job?

St. Patrick's Day

Catch a Leprechaun

Those leprechauns are sneaky and hard to catch, and they can make big ole messes too! But if you catch one, you'll get some gold or other riches! A few days before St. Patrick's Day, have your kids create some traps around the house to see if they can catch a leprechaun. The toddlers will need to set up the traps before they go to sleep, and they should check them in the morning to see if they've caught anything. Shoeboxes, large containers or mixing bowls, or even sheets can work. While the children are sleeping, leave small signs that leprechauns have been nearby, including some gold pieces (plastic, chocolate coins, and bubble-gum coins), green glitter trails, or just a big mess! Sometimes, on the morning of St. Patrick's Day, kids may find some telltale signs that they got really, really close to catching a leprechaun—such as a four-leaf clover, green beads or a necklace, or other trinkets. Better luck next year!

Four-leaf Clovers

Everyone knows that finding a four-leaf clover means good luck. Why not have your toddler create some good luck charms for everyone she loves? A four-leaf clover is easily created by folding green construction paper into fourths and then cutting a simple heart design. (Try a few samples first to get that perfect pattern.) To keep the shape together, be sure that the section where the paper will join the stem remains uncut. Before unfolding, snip off a tiny end to make a small hole where the paper is joined, and then place a green chenille pipe cleaner through the hole. (Place a small piece of tape or floral wrap tape underneath the paper where it meets the chenille stem to keep it from sliding down, and then trim or fold the chenille pipe cleaner to the desired length.) A touch of glitter spray provides that extra touch of Irish magic! Poke the clovers into some foam and let your youngster enjoy passing out good luck to teachers, family members, friends, and neighbors!

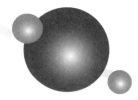

Leprechaun Sandwich Bites

Add green food coloring to peanut butter and spread it on bread. Cut sandwiches into fourths—or even better, cut them into shamrocks using a cookie cutter. Add other green side dishes as desired, such as leprechaun dip (add green food coloring to ranch dressing) served with broccoli and carrots.

St. Paddy's Pudding

Add green food coloring to a batch of vanilla pudding for a special treat, or let kids make individual servings in a plastic bag.

Ingredients
- 1 tablespoon instant pistachio pudding (or vanilla pudding with a few drops of green food coloring)
- ½ cup milk
- sandwich-size plastic bag

Put the ingredients in the bag and let kids squeeze and shake it. The pudding is ready to eat once it turns thick. If time allows, refrigerate the mix briefly to improve the taste.

April Fool's Day

Identity Exchange

Switch identities (over breakfast is a good time) for some family fun. Agree on which roles everyone will play and what responsibilities they will be in charge of. Your toddler might like acting like dad, and you can act like your toddler! It's good for a few laughs!

Practical Jokes

This can be a fun day to celebrate, as long as the pranks are good-natured practical jokes that make people laugh! Start a tradition with your kids of playing fun practical jokes on them, such as putting a gummy worm in their morning pancake, or serving them a "drink" that is really a glass of Jell-O (poured into a drinking glass with a straw added, refrigerated until set, and then served). Just make sure no hurt feelings result!

Earth Day

Mother Earth

Create an earth picture using a paper plate.

Materials

- paper plate
- crayons or markers
- water
- figurines or pictures representing things found on earth (on both land and water)
- glue

Show your toddler a simple illustration of earth. Using that as a guide, have her create her own earth by coloring the paper plate blue and green. (For very young children, adults can draw on continents and let kids color the land green and water blue.) To help kids understand the difference between land and water, have them glue on small, simple items (figurines or pictures) such as fish, dolphins, and boats in the water areas and trees and animals on the continents.

Easter

Bunny Footprints

Fashion some bunny-style footprints from paper, and on Easter morning lay out prints leading to various points in the house where special treats are hidden, culminating in an Easter basket—just in time for an egg hunt! Your toddler will love tracking the prints!

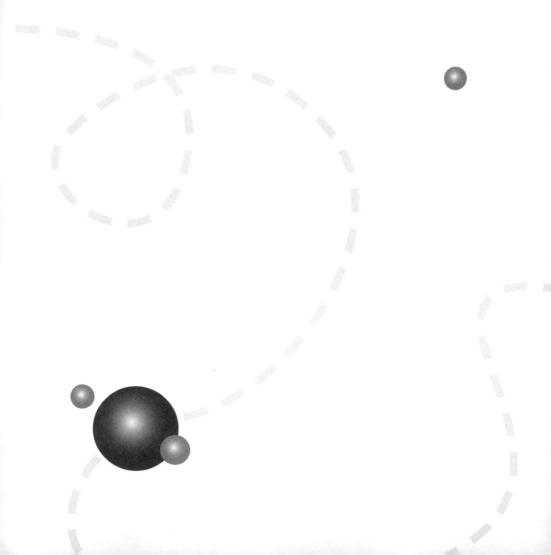

Duck Feet

Make a fun duck out of a footprint.

Materials
- 1 sheet each of white or yellow paper (or foam paper)
- pencil
- tissue paper cut into small squares
- google eyes
- craft glue
- scissors

Trace your child's foot on paper (any color) and cut out the shape. Glue the paper foot onto another piece of paper; the heel will become the top of the duck. Have your toddler glue pieces of tissue all over the footprint to form duck feathers. Glue on google eyes and then draw on a beak and feet. A variation to this activity is to cut out or trace a duck shape on a piece of paper and have your youngster glue colored feathers onto it. Feathers can be found at most craft stores. If you dare, let them use glitter glue for the beak area and glue on a button or bead for the eye.

Egg Finder Game

Hide an egg when your child is not watching and then ask him to find it. The only assistance you can provide is to quack softly when your toddler gets close to the egg and then more and more softly the more distant he becomes. You can even act like a duck and flap with excitement when the egg is found. Next, let your toddler hide the egg from you!

Cinco de Mayo

Learn Spanish

Teach youngsters the names of colors, days of the week, simple household things, or how to count to 10 in Spanish. Practice in the week leading up to Cinco de Mayo (Spanish for "Fifth of May"), and celebrate the Mexican national holiday that more and more people in the United States celebrate every year.

Mexican Hat Dance

You don't need a sombrero to do a hat dance; any hat will do! Simply crank up some Mexican-inspired music and teach kids how to dance around the hat. This fun activity also teaches kids to appreciate this style of music and encourages their sense of rhythm.

Mother's Day

Bountiful Bouquet

Surprise mom or grandma on Mother's Day with this simple and quick craft featuring kids' faces on flowers. Mom can also celebrate by making this keepsake with the kids. Either way, this is a special gift that is sure to bring a smile to the recipient's face!

Materials

- drinking straws (pick the ones with flexible necks, if available)
- cupcake liners in assorted colors
- photos featuring your kids
- green construction paper
- scissors
- glue
- paint
- glitter
- markers or other decorating items of your choice
- colored vase or short glass

Cut a photo sized to match the circle portion of a cupcake liner and glue the photo inside the liner so that the sides of the liner become the outside of the flower. (You can cut and trim the liner to create petals if you like.) You can create one flower, or you can make several showing different children or scenes. Glue a straw to the back of the cupcake liner. (For straws with flexible necks, put the bendable end closer to the flower for easy positioning.) Create a couple of leaves from green construction paper and glue them to the straw below the flower. Arrange the flowers in the vase or glass you have selected. (Trim the straw if the flower is too long to stand upright.)

Flowerpot Feet and Hands

Honor grandma or mom with a special flowerpot decorated with handprints and footprints! Tempera paint makes this easy and fun. Have kids add thumbprints around the rim for extra decorating flair. Sign the bottom and then fill the pot with soil and a favorite plant or flower!

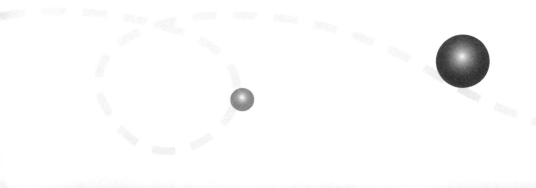

Father's Day

Dad Snack Attack

Your child can make dad his very own snack pack. Label a container (such as a plastic food storage container, an empty whipped cream tub with the label removed, or even a gift bag lined with plastic wrap or a large bag) with the word "DAD" and have your toddler use markers to decorate it. Fill it with cereal mix, pretzels, nuts, crackers, and any other treats dad loves, and mix it together. He might even share!

Father's Day Coupons

Dad or gramps can be hard to buy or make gifts for, but he's sure to appreciate some special help from or time with a loving toddler! Have toddlers create a coupon book and decorate each page. Use full-size pages or coupon-size sheets stapled together with a cover that your toddler colors or stamps handprints on. Ideas for coupons include a back rub, an afternoon together playing a sport he loves, an undisturbed afternoon nap, one sleep-in on Saturday morning, and perhaps a daddy-child outing.

King of the Castle

Let dad be king of the castle with his very own toddler-inspired royal crown. Create a simple crown out of construction paper or foam paper by drawing a shape that your child can then cut out easily with toddler-safe scissors. An easy and fun design uses a basic zigzag pattern cut across the top of a rectangular length of paper. If your child is too young to have mastered cutting with scissors, an adult should cut it out. Be sure to measure the correct circumference so it is large enough to fit on dear dad. Once the crown is cut out (remember, the sillier or more original the better), lay it out flat and let your child decorate it with markers, stickers, or whatever decorative items you have around the house. Then tape or staple the ends of the paper to form the crown. Have your child place the royal crown on dad's head. Tie a towel around his neck as a robe. You can snap a photo with dad and his subjects (kids) as a humorous keepsake.

Macaroni Heart Photo Frame

Looking for something a little different and definitely "kid-produced" for Father's Day? Your child will enjoy making this quick-and-easy photo frame for dad. The craft can be adapted for other holidays or occasions by using red, pink, and white colors for Valentine's Day, or cutting the plate into an egg shape for spring or Easter, a pumpkin shape for fall, or even a snowflake shape for Winter.

Materials:

- dinner-size paper plate cut
- macaroni noodles of shape according to preference (heart-shaped macaroni is sometimes available at stores)
- kid craft glue
- paint, glitter or even spray paint (if parents use it) in colors of choice
- wallet-size photo of child
- scissors
- tape

Cut dinner plate into a heart shape and cut out a smile heart or circle in the middle that is the right size for the child's photo to be seen. (Don't place the photo yet; just make sure the size of the cut-out is correct.) Let the child glue macaroni noodles all over the plate for decorations, then use glue, spray paint, or regular paint to create a fancy frame. When dry, simply tape the photo of the child on the back along with the tot's name and date.

Fourth of July

Fireworks Eruption

Of course, this is not *really* a fireworks eruption, but kids will shriek with delight at this awesome soda eruption, which exceeds 15 feet or more. Expect to hear lots of cheers and oohs and aahs!

Materials
- 2-liter bottle of carbonated soda (diet cola performs better and brand does not matter)
- 1 roll of Mentos or Certs (candy mints)

Go outside to a large open area (park setting or field is preferred). Make sure that your child stands 20 feet away from the soda bottle at all times. Open the bottle of soda and position it to ensure that it will not tip over. *Simultaneously* drop about 4–6 mints into the open 2-liter bottle (a big eruption will not occur if you drop them in one at a time) and get away quickly. Consider rolling a small piece of paper into the mouth of the bottle so that the mints can be dropped in more easily and you can move out of the way faster. Plan for an encore request and have more than one bottle on hand!

Patriotic Ice Cube Creations

Make red and blue drinks (such as Kool-Aid) and pour into ice cube trays. For a special Fourth of July treat, place the frozen cubes in water or a clear carbonated drink for red, white, and blue fun!

Trike/Bike Parade

Have youngsters show off their patriotic pride with a Fourth of July bike/trike parade. Half of the fun is decorating, and it doesn't matter if they're the only attraction around! Accessorizing can be as simple as wrapping red, white, and blue crepe paper around the bike or tying balloons and cut-out stars to the handlebars and all around the bike. Make a star hat for your toddler by attaching colorful star shapes around a paper headband and dress him in patriotic-themed clothes. And don't forget to have adoring fans wave the grand ole flag as the parade commences!

Halloween

Boo Your Neighbors

Create some neighborly fun this Halloween by "booing" some neighbors. First you and your toddler put together a mix of inexpensive goodies in a container or bag. Enclose an "I've been boo'd" sign of your own making (computer art, handmade, or whatever). Start the "booing" by secretly leaving the goodies with two neighbors (ring the doorbell and run so that they'll see the treats and not you!), and include these instructions: (1) Enjoy your treats!; (2) Please place your BOO sign on your front door or window; (3) Within 24 hours please copy this twice and make two treat bags and two BOO signs; secretly deliver to two neighbors who don't have a BOO sign; and (4) If you don't wish to participate, please place the BOO sign on your front door so neighbors won't think you're being ignored.

"Booing" is sure to become a neighborhood tradition, and your child will have lots of fun keeping the secret that your family started it!

Broom Ride

Calling all witches and warlocks! Grab a broom or two and have your youngster join you on a bewitching ride. Soar high and low, round corners, and pretend to sail above treetops into the night sky. Swoosh down by a local park and then twirl into a spin! Show your toddler how you control the direction of the broom by aiming high or low, tilting to one side and then the other, and then, most importantly, point out where you want to stop for a cackling refreshment stop!

Goblin's Teeth

Show your toddler how to bite off the white tip of candy corn (eating the orange and yellow part, of course). Collect the white ends in a bag and tell everyone they are "goblin's teeth."

Monster Parade

Invite playmates to create nonscary monster costumes made out of household items (no purchased costumes allowed). Then, before the play date, assemble for your toddler a homemade costume that can be easily worn with young friends. Some of the best and most original ideas incorporate a simple shirt and sweatpants and maybe a hat with embellishments. Ideas to get rolling include cookie monster, string monster, book monster, web monster, button monster, and even balloon monster. Plan to have kids debut their creations with a simple "monster parade." Don't forget the camera!

Thanksgiving

Neighborly Cheer

Establish a tradition of baking and distributing treats to your neighbors prior to the Thanksgiving holiday. Spend an afternoon with your kids making sugar cookies and decorating them. Decorate paper plates as desired with markers, glitter, or stickers. Wrap the cookies in cellophane and place on plates. Add a note telling the recipients why they are special and why you are thankful to be part of the neighborhood. Deliver them in person for some unexpected, but much appreciated, cheer.

Thankful List

Does your toddler understand the virtue of appreciation or thankfulness? Develop a list of things your youngster is thankful for. It's normal to have a toddler initially list possessions, so you can include those first. Then suggest things he may never have really thought about: having a home, food on the table, and friends, for example. A week before Thanksgiving, talk about ways to express appreciation.

Turkey Handprint Cookies

Trace your child's handprint on a piece of paper. Use that paper as a pattern to cut handprint-shaped cookies out of a batch of cookie dough. Bake as directed and cool. Now comes the fun! Have your toddler decorate the cookie like a turkey by turning the fingers into tail feathers and the thumb into the neck and head. Use an M&M or chocolate chip for the eye, a small piece of licorice or candy string to make a mouth, and use sprinkles or colored icing for the rest of the feathers.

Christmas

Elf Watch

Start a family tradition by introducing an elf-like character (for example, a toy doll or stuffed animal wearing an elf hat) to your family right after Thanksgiving. Have the new guest arrive at your front door in a package. The elf should be placed somewhere high in the home to watch over the toddlers on behalf of Santa. Make it more interesting by moving the elf from place to place and room to room and letting kids hunt for him. The elf can leave small treats, appear with a notepad and pencil nearby, or leave a trail of glitter. On Christmas Day he disappears, only to reappear the next year for another holiday season of watching kids to determine whether they've been naughty or nice!

Glitter Pinecone

Sparkly pinecones look great displayed in a basket around the holidays.

Materials

- pinecones (quantity depends on you)
- craft glue
- plastic gallon-sized resealable bags filled with glitter (use traditional red and green or perhaps gold and silver)

Have your toddler begin decorating the pinecones by applying glue over the ridges and ends. Then have her drop the pinecone into the glitter, close the bag, and shake it. Make several of these and display them around the house.

Holiday Toy Drive

Holidays often mean gifts of toys and other items for youngsters. Why not start a family tradition of giving? Using the idea that one has to give before one can receive, have a toy and clothing drive in your own home. Go through all the toys that your kids have outgrown or no longer play with. Explain to them that with the holidays coming up, they'll be receiving presents, and they should share some of their treasures with others, too. If possible, take kids in person to give a donation; if not, think of ways to instill the gift of giving.

Jingle Bell Bracelets

Pipe cleaners in red, green, or sparkly gold or silver tones coupled with some small jingle bells are all it takes for a quick and simple craft. Have your toddler string some jingle bells onto a pipe cleaner. Twist it closed around your child's wrist and trim it for size. Toddlers may love the sound so much they will want one for each wrist and ankle!

Reindeer Antlers

Expect endearing comments when your toddler proudly shows off his charming antlers. No two antler hats are ever the same, because this quick and easy-to-make design features the uniqueness of your child's hands.

Materials

- 2 sheets of fun foam (preferred for durability, but construction paper or even plain white paper will also work)
- pen or marker to trace around child's fingers
- stapler or tape
- glitter glue (or glue stick and glitter of choice)
- scissors

Cut a brown foam sheet lengthwise into a 2-inch strip to fit snugly around your child's head. (It may take two strips affixed together for larger kids.) Have your child decorate the band if desired. An adult can also write a child's name or the name of the "reindeer" he is about to become. Then staple or tape the band to size. Trace around your child's hands (fingers apart) on either a brown sheet or, if preferred, a contrasting color. An adult should cut out the hand shapes. Kids should then decorate the hands (now "antlers") with some sparkly glitter or other colorful accents. Once the antlers are complete and dry, an adult should staple them to either side of the band. Kids will magically become part of Santa's sleigh team just in time for Christmas!

Reindeer Food

Everyone remembers to put cookies and milk out for Santa each year, but what about the hard-working team of reindeer? Before your cherubs go to sleep on Christmas Eve, have them sprinkle some magical reindeer food on the front lawn or by the front door so the team can keep its energy up to make it to all the boys' and girls' homes before morning!

Ingredients
- oatmeal
- "magic reindeer dust" (gold or brightly colored glitter)

Put the ingredients in a snack-sized bag. Shake it up, and it's ready to give to youngsters to put out before going to bed. The magic dust will glisten in the snow or grass, making it easy for the reindeer to spot. If you live in an area where you are concerned about wildlife eating the glitter, substitute bakery sprinkles or even sugar (colored with food color, if desired).

Rudolph Candy Cane

This is a quick and simple craft that kids can make for their playmates, with only a little help from an adult.

Materials

- individually wrapped candy canes (you pick size and flavor)
- 2 wiggle eyes for each reindeer (5 mm size works great)
- very small red pom-poms (one for each reindeer, for Rudolph's nose, of course!)
- 18-inch pipe cleaners (any color is fine, but metallic silver or gold is really catchy)
- tiny jingle bells
- craft glue

Glue eyes on the rounded (hook) part of the candy cane. Glue red pom-pom "noses" onto the cane below the eyes. To make a jingle-jangle reindeer collar, cut a 3-inch or 4-inch segment of pipe cleaner (see what works best for the candy cane and your toddler's hands), then slide the pipe cleaner through the opening of a jingle bell. Fasten it to the cane by twisting it closed at the back. Take an uncut pipe cleaner and twist it around the top of the cane (make both ends of equal length) to form simple antlers.

Santa Hat

Your toddler will have hours of "ho ho ho's" with this quick and easy paper hat.

Materials
- red construction paper
- scissors
- white cotton balls
- glue
- glitter
- stapler
- tape

Cut a red strip to fit around a child's head and tape or staple it closed. Next cut out a hat shape (using a basic triangle shape works best). Write your child's name in glue on the front center of the hat, and let your child sprinkle glitter on the glue to create a sparkly name. When dry, tape or staple the "hat" part to the front of the red strip, creating a basic Santa hat design. Now it's time to decorate with cotton balls. Use glue dabs and let your toddler place cotton balls on the base section of the hat and then do the same in a circle design at the triangle's point to create a white "ball" at the top of the hat. Here comes Santa!

Hanukkah

Dreidel

Have your toddler make a dreidel. It's fun to create and makes an interesting holiday display.

Materials

- 10–12 Popsicle sticks (colored ones are best but plain will do)
- square piece of foam trimmed to the length of the Popsicle sticks
- craft glue
- markers (optional)

Have your youngster glue Popsicle sticks all around the foam square until all sides are covered. Insert one in the center of one end to make the handle. Have your child color or decorate with markers and dreidel symbols, if desired.

Handprint Menorah

Make a keepsake Menorah out of handprints.

Materials
- 1 sheet of construction paper (or foam paper for durability) in color of choice for candle base
- 1 sheet of yellow paper (construction or foam) for flame
- scissors
- glue stick

Trace your toddler's hands on the paper selected for the candle base and cut out the shapes. Overlap the thumbs and place together. The eight fingers are the candles that represent each night of Hanukkah, and the thumbs are the one candle (called the Shamash) to light the others. Cut nine flame flickers out of the yellow paper and let your toddler glue them to the tops of the fingers. Or have your child glue on one flame each night of Hanukkah.

Kwanzaa

Beaded Necklaces

Make your own Kwanzaa-inspired beaded necklaces.

Materials

- colorful plastic line used for necklaces (available at any craft store) or yarn
- beads in Kwanzaa colors of black, red, and green (with openings large enough to be strung on the plastic line or yarn)
- scissors
- paint, if desired

Knot one end of the line so that beads will not slip through. Have toddlers thread the beads and then tie the ends together when complete. Even though young toddlers may not be old enough to understand the meaning, recipients will like the color strands, which represent black for the people, red for their struggles, and green for hope and a bright future.

Kwanzaa Principles

Kwanzaa is a seven-day African American holiday that celebrates the harvest. It takes place from December 26 through January 1. Its name comes from Swahili, an African language. The seven principles of Kwanzaa, which can be simplified to be more age appropriate for toddlers' understanding, are (1) love of family (unity); (2) doing your best (self-determination); (3) responsibility; (4) working together (cooperative economics); (5) dreams for the future (purpose); (6) having an imagination (creativity); and (7) faith. Your family can become stronger and more connected by discussing what each of these principles means. Each night of Kwanzaa, have each member talk about a way they can contribute a particular trait during the upcoming year.

Indoor Activities

3

Harness your toddler's endless energy with inside adventures, arts and crafts, games, and kitchen fun.

Airplane Adventure

Toddlers will love packing their bags and pretending to soar through the sky bound for some exciting destination! Once the passengers present their tickets to the gate agent, board the plane, and fasten their seat belts, you can take on the personality of the airplane itself by extending your arms, taking off, leveling out, showing passengers scenic sites (check out those mountains and clouds!), and, finally, coming in for a landing.

Apple Jigsaw Puzzle

Create some edible fun by carving an apple into a very simple jigsaw puzzle. Cut the apple into large, puzzle-like pieces (5–6 pieces work well) and then put it back together. Have your toddler take the apple apart and then reassemble it before taking that first healthy bite!

Art Gallery Corner

Your toddler makes many extraordinary artistic creations, but instead of just displaying them on the refrigerator, select the best ones for your toddler's own art gallery! Choose a place in your home where artwork can be tacked up or even framed and hung. Clustering pieces of art, especially when made with different mediums, can help encourage a budding artist and be a conversation piece too!

Beary Nice Day

Proclaim a certain day "Bear Day." Have your toddler invite her bear friends for a snack, and serve Teddy Grahams with "bear juice." Before the guests arrive, create a bear crown for the hostess. Make this by having her color a picture of a bear (creative parents can simply draw a bear face on paper and have their toddler color it), cut it out, and glue it to a paper band that is cut to fit around the child's head.

Box of Dreams

Have your toddler create her very own "box of dreams" that she can look at and keep by her bed or in a cherished location. A shoe box works great, but any box will do. Start by decorating the box based on your youngster's interests. Or wrap it in black paper (an adult will need to do this) and have your toddler decorate it with star stickers, glitter, and perhaps the moon. If your child wants to become a ballerina, find pictures of ballerinas from magazines to put in the box. A race car driver? Maybe a few toy cars can be included. An astronaut? How about tucking in some star shapes and a toy rocket or astronaut action figure? Encourage your toddler to look at the prized contents every few weeks and make changes as desired.

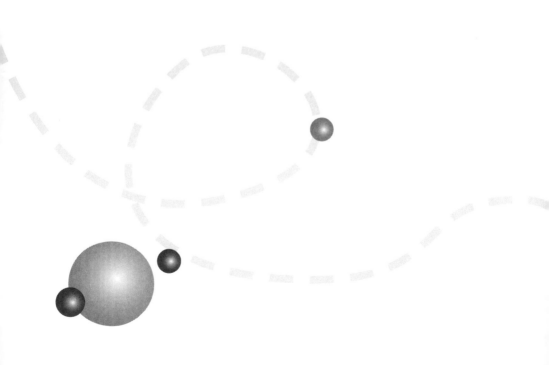

Bubble Wizard

The next time a toddler takes a bath, pour in an extra-generous supply of bubble bath and make some zany bubble creations (parent supervised, of course!). Encourage creating bears, mustaches, crowns, long hair, body armor, or just a silly bubble face. Have a hand mirror available so your little wizard can see her creations! Add to the fun by having her make up a story as she goes along, perhaps changing the bubble creations to reflect different characters. If your child is hesitant about creating stories, make one up for her or read a favorite ahead of time and "act out" the story in the bathtub! You'll have the cleanest toddler around!

Cardboard Creations

Many stores are happy to give away cardboard boxes from large appliances or furniture if you ask for them. Request one or two and then transform them into a tent, race car, puppet theater, robot, or castle! Parents should take their cue from toddlers about what they want, and then be the ones to cut out windows, create a drawbridge, or help with other elements. Let kids decorate the box with markers or kid-friendly paint; if desired, wrap the box with paper and let them draw on it.

Cat's Meow

You and your toddler can become barnyard cats for an afternoon. First, choose what color or type of cat you want to be and pick a cat name. Pretend to stretch, preen, chase mice, and curl up on a soft pillow. See if you can communicate in cat language. Extend your claws and pretend to scratch. Practice purring!

Container Mystery

Divide your toddler's toys into several containers and allow him to choose and play with the toys in one container at a time. Limit a container "discovery" to once a week or so. Too many toys overwhelm a child, and half the fun is playing with something "new" or rediscovered.

Crazy Glasses

Who would have thought some pipe cleaners could create so much fun? In this activity use them to create eyeglasses for toddlers. Consider a bright-colored mixture to fashion rainbow glasses, make round lenses with black pipe cleaners to look like Harry Potter, or add accents to the frames to create a unique, zany pair. This is a good activity for when a classmate or friend gets glasses of his own.

Dance Recital

Hang a sheet in a doorway to make a stage curtain, gather clothing items that could become a costume, pop in some kid-friendly tunes, and let your child dance away! You can serve as the master of ceremonies and introduce the child to an imaginary audience. For special fun set up a video camera and film your starlet for lots of laughs at later viewing.

Date Nights

Plan a standing "date night" with your child for quality one-on-one time. An activity can be as simple as a walk in the neighborhood, movie-watching and snuggle time, or breakfast in the backyard. Let your child help with planning and be sure to keep your part of the bargain by providing your child with your uninterrupted and undivided attention!

Dinosaur Food
(No-bake Cookie Recipe)

Kids like to cook and help out in the kitchen. This fun, simple, and quick recipe that toddlers can make (mostly) by themselves encourages their fascination with dinosaurs, and, even better, the ingredients are typically found in most pantries!

Ingredients

- ⅛ cup of dirt (cocoa)
- ¼ cup swamp water (milk)
- 1 cup crushed bones (sugar)
- 1 cup dino fat (butter)
- 1 cup grass (uncooked oatmeal)
- ¼ cup squashed bugs (peanut butter)

Mix dirt, swamp water, crushed bones, and fat in a saucepan. Cook 5–10 minutes. Remove from heat and stir in grass and squashed bugs. Drop by teaspoonfuls onto waxed paper. Let cool and eat. Makes 2–3 dozen.

Door Hanger Art

With a simple piece of foam paper or heavy paper (such as poster board), your child can create a door hanger for outside his room. Simply cut a 4-inch by 6-inch piece of paper, then punch a hole in each top corner and tie a string long enough to fit over the door handle. Then let your youngster have fun decorating it! Suggestions include foam shapes or letters, stickers, glitter glue, or whatever sparks your toddler's imagination. Parents can write a message such as "A Princess Sleeps Here" or "Beware: You're Entering Timmy's Pirate Den." For extra fun decorate the other side with a different message and let your toddler choose which side to display.

Face-off

Sit crisscross style across from each other and have a face-off! Your toddler begins by making a funny face that you have to copy in return. Then you create one for your youngster to mimic. There's just one catch: whoever laughs first has to get up and run around in a circle (or do 10 jumping jacks or whatever you choose) before starting the game again!

Family Coins

It's important to teach kids the value of coins and their various denominations, but wouldn't it be fun to let kids create their own family coins? Cut circles of different sizes out of heavy paper (poster board) and let kids decorate them with faces of various family members, add glitter or other designs, and choose their value. Consider using actual photographs of family members to decorate the coins. Craft a special coin box for safekeeping of these priceless treasures.

Food Dye Experiments

Isn't it fascinating how a squirt of food dye can change water, icing, and many other things in the kitchen into something else? Introduce your youngsters to the magic of food dye and how mixing colors can create something new. Consider letting them dip eggs into food dye (even when it's NOT Easter). They'll love experimenting!

Footprint Butterflies

These gorgeous creations will be special keepsakes of your toddler's feet and also make great gifts for grandparents!

Materials

- paper (foam sheet, poster board, or plain paper)
- decorating items of choice (glitter, stickers, etc.)
- pipe cleaners
- glue
- google eyes (optional)

Trace your child's footprint on the paper. Cut out two wing shapes and let your toddler have fun decorating them with glitter, foam shapes, stickers, etc. Turn the footprint upside down and glue the wings to the middle of it. Bend the pipe cleaners in half and curl the ends; glue them to the heel of the footprint and to the wings. Then glue google eyes to the heel part of the print and draw a smile with a glitter pen. Let dry and enjoy your footprint butterfly! (Be sure to sign and date it on the back.)

Glass Music

Teach your kids how to make music with glasses filled with various amounts of water. Choose an assortment of 3–4 glasses, fill with various amounts of water, and then either blow gently across the top or try making sounds by wetting a finger and rubbing it in a fast circular motion around the rim. Your toddlers will be fascinated by the different sounds you can make when you change the amount of water in the glass.

Nail Shop

Let your toddler "polish" your fingernails and toenails with a paintbrush and water (or dab in some water-based paint and some glitter for color if you're really daring!).

I Did It! Board

Find a place in the house (refrigerator, window, or hall-way) where you can create a weekly "I Did It!" board. Toddlers learn so many amazing things every week, and it's nice to be recognized for them! Each Sunday write the week's date (e.g., "July 8–14") and your child's name on the board. List any new accomplishments as they occur. At the end of the week, discuss the things learned, offer praise, and start a new week! Consider keeping a scrapbook of past weeks that can be reviewed together at the end of the year!

Indoor Hopscotch

Hopscotch can be a fun and safe way to play indoors! Simply mark off hopscotch squares on the floor with masking tape, number the spaces, and get ready for action! When done simply remove the tape and your house is back to normal. (Be sure to test the tape on a small, out-of-the-way section of the floor to make sure it leaves no unpleasant marks.)

Key Keeper

Kids love keys and the whole concept of locking and unlocking things. Purchase an inexpensive kid's lock and key set and put the key on a lanyard or a coiled key-holder bracelet (or simply make a necklace with string or ribbon). Attach the lock to something of significance for the child and let him have the responsibility of locking and unlocking it and keeping the key safe. Kids may like locking up the carrying case for their toy cars, their doll tote, or some other container of prized possessions (just make sure you have a way to open the lock in case the key is lost). To avoid losing the key, choose a designated spot (such as a peg on the wall) that serves as a key holder when the key is not being worn. Praise your child for being responsible with the key over a period of time.

Living Room Rodeo

Yee haw! It's rodeo time in your home, and all you need is some enthusiasm and a willing body! Start with a contestant parade into the arena, and then begin the competition, complete with barrel racing around the kitchen, bronco and bull riding exhibitions, calf tying with a favorite stuffed animal and a shoelace, and steer wrestling, too. Your youngster will earn the crown of rodeo queen or king!

Magical Maze

Turn your house into a magical maze using some sheets, towels, furniture, and your imagination! Create tunnels and barriers by hanging towels and sheets over pieces of furniture. Your maze can be located in one room or be spread across your home. It is completely up to you how much time, effort, and supplies you want to use!

Measurement Mania

Who knew that a ruler could provide entertainment? Give your toddler a ruler and let him measure things. It's great for teaching numbers and the concepts of large and small. He'll feel like a big kid checking measurements, and even if he's too small to really "get" the concept, he'll have fun pretending. Adults can help small toddlers by recording findings or labeling things being measured (a chair, a dog bowl, a foot, etc.) for easy reference in the future.

My Growth Chart

Find a discreet wall or door frame somewhere in your home or garage where kids can easily stand, be measured, and see for themselves how tall they are. Mark a line showing their height and be sure to date it. (Go ahead and use a marker or pen; you can always paint over it later.) Remeasure every 3–4 months. If you have more than one child, use different colors. The kids will love seeing how they are growing and how little they used to be!

Pack 'n' Play

Pick an imaginary destination and have your child pack for the trip. If he has his own suitcase or duffel bag, have him use that. Otherwise, any type of bag will be just fine. Help your youngster plan by going over what things he uses throughout the day (pj's, toothbrush, change of clothes, etc.). Toddlers like thinking through a trip and what will be needed. Talk with them about what would happen if they forgot to pack something important, like shoes, for example!

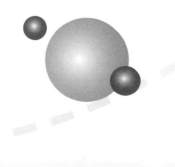

Penny Jar Savings

Adults may be annoyed by pennies, but kids love them! Why not turn them into an incentive and a savings plan? Create a simple penny bank by using a plain glass jar. Remove the label and cut a slit in the jar's lid so kids can drop the pennies in. (The clear glass works best so kids can see their savings grow!)

Pick-up Party

Whoever said that cleaning up has to be no fun? Turn up some kid-friendly tunes and have a "pick-up party." Drive those toy cars back to their garages while dancing, turning, and hopping. Dolls can be swinging partners while getting put away. Dirty clothes can be jump shots into the laundry basket, and toothpaste can be cleaned up with a twirl and a smile. It's so much fun, your kids will want to pick up like this more often!

Pint-sized Kitchen

Using boxes or even a dedicated space in a cabinet, create a mini kitchen area for your toddler. Provide him with his own set of mixing bowls, measuring spoons, and other basic items so he can pretend to cook right alongside mom or dad. A box can be transformed into a stove or refrigerator. Add a chef's apron for extra fun!

Pizza Chef

With just a few simple ingredients, let your child show off her culinary genius with an easy homemade pizza masterpiece for family or friends.

Ingredients
- croissant rolls
- spaghetti sauce, tomato sauce, or pizza sauce
- cheese
- pizza toppings of choice

Have your toddler roll out croissant dough and press it onto a pizza pan or cookie sheet; pinch up edges to form a crust. Spread on some spaghetti sauce or tomato sauce. Top with cheese (this is often kids' favorite part). Next, have her add her favorite pizza toppings. Then bake according to the croissant cooking instructions. Your toddler will feel like a gourmet chef. For extra fun, create a pizza portrait using pepperoni slices for eyes, cheese for hair, olives for ears, etc. Once the pizza has cooled, show your toddler how to cut it with a pizza wheel (if you have one). The whole family can enjoy!

Play-Doh® Architecture

Play-Doh and toothpicks can create hours of fun. Show toddlers how to roll small pieces of Play-Doh into balls. Connect the pieces to each other using either flat-end craft toothpicks (nonpointy) or stir sticks (used for coffee). Create stars, space stations, hotels, and more!

Rubber Duckies

Purchase a few inexpensive rubber ducks and float them in a bathroom sink. Secretly number the bottom of each and assign the number to a fun activity or treat! Let your youngster pick a duck and view the bottom, and award her the prize!

Sign Language Basics

Teach your child how to sign his name and practice some basic sign language symbols. Sign language is a practical skill that can help young toddlers and kids with language disorders to communicate, and learning the letters is also lots of fun! If you don't know sign language, you can easily find a basic alphabet chart at a local library or by searching on the Internet.

Sponge Friend

Who hasn't heard of SpongeBob SquarePants and his sidekick Patrick? Your kids will enjoy making and then bathing with handcrafted versions of these two characters, made simply from—you guessed it—sponges!

Materials

- 2 inexpensive, large, plain rectangular sponges
- wiggle eyes or buttons
- permanent markers
- glue that will hold when in water

Making a sponge friend is super simple! Just glue on google eyes (or sew on buttons for eyes), and use permanent marker to draw on a nose and mouth (and clothes, if desired). Cut the second sponge into the shape of another sea friend and affix the face as above. Your toddler will beg to take a bath!

Stretch 'n' Grow

Simple exercises are great for toddlers, and let's face it, for adults too! Create a simple routine (toe touches, jumping jacks, stretches, and jogging in place), and you'll both be more fit and alert as a result!

Tambourine Magic

Let your child practice keeping the beat to songs or create a unique rhythm with a homemade tambourine.

Materials

- 2 paper plates
- cotton or newspaper
- hole puncher
- string or yarn
- small jingle bells
- decorations (stickers, glitter, crayons, etc.)

Have your child decorate the bottom of both plates with markers, paint, crayons, stickers (or whatever you have available). Place the two plates together (decorated sides out) and fill the space between them using cotton or newspaper. Punch holes about 2 inches apart all the way around the plates, and have your youngster string them together as a lacing activity. Last, attach jingle bells to each set of holes using string or yarn. Let the music begin!

Temporary Tattoos

Draw temporary tattoos on each other's legs or upper arms with washable markers.

This Toddler's Got Talent!

Did you know your toddler could do a front somersault? Or touch his toes while keeping his knees straight? Do the splits? Wow! Your kid's got a lot of talent! Have a show-off session, with you serving as the emcee calling out ideas for him to perform. Your youngster will like being the star!

Thumbprint Peacock

Paint your toddler's hand in kid-friendly blue paint and make a handprint on construction paper. (The thumb part of the handprint will become the head and neck of the peacock.) Then using a complementary color (purple or green works well), have her make thumbprints at the top of the thumb and each finger to resemble the peacock's head and four feather plumes. Add some eyes and a smile to the peacock's face, and you've got a thumbprint masterpiece!

Train Crossing

Teach your youngster how locomotive engineers use train whistle patterns as a way to communicate. The most common one—two long blasts, one short, then one long—signifies that a train is approaching a grade crossing. Use your arm to make a gate that lowers to stop cars from crossing and have your toddler act like the train, making the pattern of two long, one short, and then one long before passing through.

Treasure Map Adventure

Surprise a toddler one unhurried morning with a simple hand-drawn treasure map made of construction paper, rolled up and tied with a ribbon. The map should depict simple symbols and an "X" over an obvious location (refrigerator, chair, dog bowl) to indicate treasure. The map should bear the child's name and be placed where it will be easily spotted. Ahoy, matey, it's a map for a treasure hunt! You might have to help your toddler with the clues and what to do next, but he'll quickly catch on. When the location is figured out, another rolled-up map with a clue awaits! After four or five locations, leave a small surprise (a treat, a family movie to watch, bubbles, or a new book) for your child. This unexpected adventure will surely inspire pleas for future treasure hunts and bounties!

Wastebasket Ball

All you need is a wastebasket and some wadded-up paper for great toddler fun! Let kids practice their trash basketball prowess by lobbing in a few shots. Increase the challenge by moving the wastebasket farther and farther away.

Western Dancing

Even the youngest of toddlers can learn simple steps and motions such as a basic two-step or three-step. Older kids would love learning a line dance. Don't know any? Make one up and have your own unique family dance.

Wishing Star

Sometimes toddlers have difficulties sitting still long enough to see a shooting star in the vast night sky. Therefore, have your child make her very own wishing star. Cut a star pattern on heavy paper, color and decorate it (sparkly glitter is always a big hit), and then pin it on the ceiling of her room! She can make wishes on it whenever she chooses!

Yoga

Relaxation isn't just for adults; kids love to stretch and relax too, especially to start off the morning or after a busy day! Learn basic yoga positions and develop a routine to do together. Your hearts and minds will love you both for it!

Zoo Pretend Adventure

Take your youngster on a visit to the zoo without ever leaving your living room! First, on your own, find zoo animals featured in books or on the Internet. (Many zoos now have Web sites that feature interesting facts and photos of animals in their care.) Then, together, make a list of animals your toddler would like to see on an imaginary visit to the zoo. Using the books or Internet as a guide, visit the animal areas one by one and talk about each animal with your child. How tall is an adult giraffe? How big is a hippo? What is the difference between a monkey and an ape? Your kid will love hearing these fast facts about wildlife and the pretend visit will make him much more informed when he visits a zoo for real!

Outdoor Adventures

4

Backyard escapades, adventure walks, scavenger hunts, and all kinds of fun in the sun can make outdoor activities an endless source of entertainment.

Ant Observation

Ants are everywhere, and most likely you'll see an anthill somewhere near where you live or play. Keeping a safe distance, of course, show your toddler an ant's life from a people perspective. Explain the trails, how they carry food, and how there are different types of ants. If you find a trail, follow it and see where and how far it goes.

Ball Tag

Play a round or two of ball tag! The person who is "it" tries to tag people out by gently throwing a lightweight ball, like a small inflatable beach ball, at them. If tagged, that person becomes it.

Bike Road-eo

Hold a bike road-eo, either with just your child or with other kids too. A good time to organize one would be during May, Bicycle Safety Month. Arrange some cones or other items into a bicycle course and have your toddler ride around them (on a bike, trike, Big Wheel-style trike, or even a scooter). Teach her the appropriate hand signals for various maneuvers.

Bubble Blowing Adventure

Using some dish soap and objects found in the kitchen (a whisk, grater, or strainer), show your toddler how to blow bubbles. Daring folks can try this in the kitchen, but a less messy option is to take it outdoors. Turn the bubble-blowing fun into an adventure by making up stories about how the bubble is born, how it travels around to see the world, and what the bubble may encounter along the way!

Bumblebee Rocks

Youngsters can turn ordinary rocks into bumblebees in no time flat!

Materials
- flat rocks (clean and dry)
- craft paint in colors of your choice
- yellow paint for the head area
- wiggle eyes
- permanent black marker
- craft glue

Start the activity with a bumblebee rock hunt (if time permits and the right kind of rocks are available nearby). After the rocks are selected, have your child wash and dry them. Now it's time to create! An adult can help get the project started by using a permanent marker to make the head section and mark stripes a toddler can paint in. Black and yellow may be what "real" bumblebees look like, but toddlers should be urged to make bumblebees of any color combination! When paint is dry, glue on the eyes.

Buzz Stroll

Try a bumblebee stroll by having your toddler make the buzz-buzz sound of a bee, flapping arms like wings, and visiting different plants and flowers outdoors.

Car Wash

Washing the family car can be one of the most fun toddler activities around—and just look at the results! Let your toddler have a sponge with a bowl or cup of water (avoid buckets of water unless you are directly supervising at all times). Even better, turn your toddler loose with a hose and sprayer (prepare to get wet!). Another variation is to let your child pretend to drive the car through the car wash, sitting inside the vehicle as you wash it (as long as temperatures that day are not too hot). Youngsters love making faces through the window while getting soaped or sprayed with the water!

Construction Time

Let your toddler become a construction engineer by helping her build something special from materials found outdoors. Sticks, rocks, bark, and other things can be constructed into pretend buildings. Bring wooden blocks and other sturdy items outdoors to contribute to designs.

Dog Walk

Take your child for a walk at the park (or a dog park if one exists nearby) and count the number and types of dogs that you and your youngster see.

Driveway or Sidewalk Bowling

Use easy-to-knock-over items (plastic water bottles filled with dirt or some rocks at the bottom are great) to create outdoor bowling fun. Have your toddler use a small sports ball that can be rolled into a formation of "bowling pins." Whoever bowls gets to be the one to set up the pins next. It's helpful to use chalk or some other sort of marker to indicate where the pins are supposed to go. Your youngster will enjoy keeping score of how many pins are knocked over!

Fantasy Sports Star

Does your toddler dream of being a football player? Olympic ice skater? Gymnast, perhaps? Let your youngster plan and act out a role in a fantasy sport. Ask for a demonstration of a winning touchdown, an amazing jump, or landing an especially difficult tumbling move. Help your child enjoy the moment by taking photos (even pretend ones) and asking for an autograph!

Flashlight Stroll

Take an unhurried evening stroll around the neighborhood with flashlights and marvel at the sights and sounds of the night. Bring a bug-catcher or jar to temporarily collect any interesting insect finds. Take time to let your kids look at how bugs are attracted to street lights (or similar lighting) and be sure to explain why. Listen to sounds of crickets and dogs, cars driving past, and other night sounds. Let kids explore (safely, of course). A night adventure with a flashlight just begs for a repeat session!

Flashlight Tag

Whoever is "it" gets a flashlight and counts to 10 while everyone hides. If whoever is "it" shines the flashlight on a hiding player, that player becomes "it" for the next round!

Frog Jump

Have your toddler crouch with bent knees and fingers touching the ground, then leap up and extend his arms like a jumping frog. Join in, and you'll see this exercise isn't so easy! Count your leaps together, and you'll get to practice your numbers while becoming more physically fit!

Garden Creation

Let your child have his own garden area, and craft a special sign so everyone will know whose garden it is! Keep the plot small and simple; remember, even small patios or balconies can boast a large potted plant or two.

Gemstone Hunt

Wad some masking tape into nugget-sized "rocks." Paint them with gemstone-colored shades and add some glitter glue for extra accents. When the paint is dry, have a gemstone hunt in your backyard or at a park. Make some stones glittery gold and bury them just beneath the surface for a special miner's find!

Helicopter Spin

Have your toddler extend her arms out like helicopter blades and take flight. Have her spin and turn, go high and low, land, and take off again.

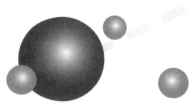

Hide the Ball

Using a fairly large ball, play hide and seek outdoors by having your toddler find the object you've hidden. Be sure not to hide something too high for a youngster's view. When she finds it, it is her turn to hide it and your turn to search!

Howl at the Moon

Teach your child some things about coyotes and their behavior. Then, after first making sure that the moon is visible, venture out and take turns howling at the moon! (Make sure it's early enough not to scare the neighbors!)

Hula Hoop Fun

Hula hoops provide hours of fun, and activities are plentiful. A hula hoop can serve as a "safe zone" boundary for game participants to stand inside, the target in which to bounce a ball, a jump rope of sorts, and, of course, simply for hula-hooping! Smaller sizes are available for little ones.

Jump Overs

Create an obstacle course for outdoor jumping. Use empty boxes, milk cartons, and other small objects (nothing that could hurt your kid) to create your course and have your child practice jumping over each object, landing on both feet. When your toddler has mastered the course, start again, but this time jumping backward!

Listening Hike

Take a silent hike and listen to the various sounds around you. Each time your toddler hears something new, have him say it, and your job is to keep count. Let him marvel at the sounds of cars, water sprinklers, lawn mowers, kids playing, and a host of other wonderful outdoor sounds.

Mailbox Count

Next time you go for a walk around the neighborhood, have your child count the number of mailboxes. See how high your toddler can count, then help him learn to count even higher.

Moon Adventure

Take a fantasy trip to the moon. Board your own rocket ship, blast off into space, and land on the moon. Look around at the surroundings. See any aliens? Ask your toddler what they look like. Are they friendly—or not? What do you do next? Have your child dig for moon rocks that you can take back to Earth. Nothing is needed here but a big imagination and some little astronauts!

Moon Magic

Create a monthly moon chart that allows youngsters to chart the cycles of the moon through easy graphic symbols. Charting the moon can be as simple as using a calendar and helping a child to draw lunar phases. Take your child outside to view the moon and see how its shape corresponds to the phases on your moon calendar.

Mud Pie Contest

Encourage your child to get dirty making a mud pie. Use any tin pie plate or plastic container to construct the pie, then ask your toddler to decorate it with flowers, grass, rocks, or anything else he can find. Have a contest to see who can create the best-looking mud pie!

Obstacle Course Challenge

Invent a noncompetitive obstacle course that involves stations or steps. (Don't make it too hard or too complicated; otherwise, kids won't want to participate.) Think simple, and use the landscape at hand. A sample course could include (1) run to this tree and then crawl around it; (2) walk backward to the sidewalk; (3) jump over this stick three times; and (4) hop to the finish line! If more than one kid is participating, have them do the obstacle course one at a time, and don't time them to determine who comes in first. Remember, everyone is a winner! Finish off with a refreshing drink and healthy snack.

Outdoor Guide

Have your toddler act as an official tour guide to the outdoors. Have him take you on an outdoor adventure, with him leading the way. Play the part of the eager student while your child teaches you all about nature!

Painting Fun

On a warm day, have kids don swimsuits and go out-doors for some body-painting fun!

Materials

- powdered tempera paints (available at most craft stores)
- 2–4 cups of baby shampoo (baby shampoo will not irri-tate toddler's eyes or skin; the amount will depend on how many colors you plan to mix)
- plastic bowls
- paint brushes (fingers can also work)

Simply mix the paints with shampoo and let the kids paint their bodies. The shampoo will cause the colors to lather, allowing for some really cool shapes and designs as well as some pretty funky hairstyles! The best part is that it comes off easily with a quick run through the sprinkler or outdoor hose, with plenty left over to try it again!

Penguin Parade

Show your kids pictures of penguins and then have them dress in black and white, don mittens on their hands, and tie pillows around their tummies. Then march (or waddle) around the yard like penguins!

Pine Cone Bird Treat

Create a tasty treat for birds and squirrels.

Materials
- 1 pine cone
- narrow ribbon or string
- peanut butter
- birdseed
- butter knife or spoon

Fasten a ribbon or string under the ridges around the top of the pine cone. Knot it with enough ribbon left for hanging. Next, have your toddler spread peanut butter all over the pine cone, then roll it in birdseed. Hang it outdoors and watch the birds and other backyard creatures enjoy a tasty treat!

Rainy Day Umbrella Fun

If it's drizzling outdoors and there's no threat of lightning, grab a few umbrellas and spend some time together in the rain! Don rain boots (or go barefoot, weather permitting) and enjoy the rainfall. Collect raindrops, splash in puddles together, twirl the umbrellas and do a rain dance, or just sit together and listen to the drops as they fall.

Red Light, Green Light

Play this childhood favorite by first designating an activity a kid needs to do (such as hopping) and then shouting "green light" (for go) and "red light" (for stop). Establish a start and finish line and play it just with your own child or as a contest with lots of kids.

Ribbon Twirl

Tie a long ribbon around a small plastic hoop or bracelet (for easy holding) and let your child dance with it outdoors in the wind. Encourage arm waving, twirling, and running with the ribbon in tow.

Sleeping Lion

Have your child curl up outside like a sleeping lion. Your job is to get him to move without touching him (tell jokes, pretend to tickle, be silly, etc.). If you can make him move or open his eyes, the roles are reversed, and you become the sleeping lion.

Sounds of Outside

Outside noises make for interesting listening and identification. Have your toddler name all the noises heard inside at home and then compare them to noises heard outside at the park or at sports practice. Compare and contrast the kinds of noises as well as their different volumes (a good concept to learn). Keep notes for your toddler so that later you can talk about what was heard in different places and to reinforce the concept of comparison and contrast.

Statue Freeze Play

Crank up the music and let your kids dance! When the music stops, they must freeze like statues. Start the music again for some wild moves. Whoever is caught moving after the music has stopped becomes the next one to start and stop the music!

Sunrise, Sunset

Invite your toddler to experience a sunrise breakfast with you. All you need is a blanket to sit on and some morning treats. Later, watch a sunset together. Ask your youngster to compare what was the same and what was different about the sunrise and the sunset. Find out whether he prefers morning or evening and create a tradition of watching the sun rise or set on a regular basis.

Three-fer Challenge

Have your child do three of something (e.g., three claps)—it doesn't matter what. Then have her add three of something else. Keep adding and see how well she can remember the pattern. Examples include three hops on one foot, followed by three claps, three jumping jacks, etc. Better watch out, though—your youngster may remember the pattern better than you!

Time Travel

Don your time-travel watch and take your toddler on a magical time-travel adventure. Enter a closet together, count to 10, and exit outdoors into another time or dimension of your tot's choosing. Explore the different world together to experience prehistoric times where dinosaurs roamed, the era of knights and princesses, or even future Earth!

Tiger Tag

Play tag with your toddler outdoors, but with a twist: all the players have to act like tigers. Pounce, growl, run through the grass, and hide. Let your youngster choose different animals to give this childhood game a fun new twist.

Toddler Ball

How many bounces can your toddler do with a big bouncy ball? Show your child how to dribble a ball, bounce and catch, and do other eye-hand coordination skills.

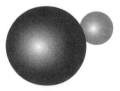

Trash Walk

One of the best ways to help your youngster learn not to litter is to have a trash walk. Arm your toddler with a small plastic bag and gloves, and the two of you pick up trash that you see along your walk. Talk about the ill effects of littering and why items should always be placed in trash cans. To avoid any potentially dangerous or unsanitary items being picked up, ask your child to scout for trash and get your okay first before it is touched.

Tree Thanks

Sit with your toddler under a nice shade tree and talk about why trees are important in nature and how they help us. Give a few examples of things made from trees and of fruits that come from trees. Later, have your child draw a picture of a tree.

Turtle Tag

Play tag with the twist that players who lie down on their backs with feet up (like an upside-down turtle) are considered safe!

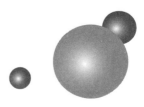

Water Balloon Throw

Fill small balloons with water, draw a target on the fence or driveway with chalk, and let your toddler have some fun. Bursting the balloons and watching the water explode out is fascinating to toddlers, and is a simple and fun activity for warm days.

Water Mister Master

Provide your toddler with his very own water mister and let him water plants outdoors. When the job is done, he can cool down by misting himself and anyone else in sight!

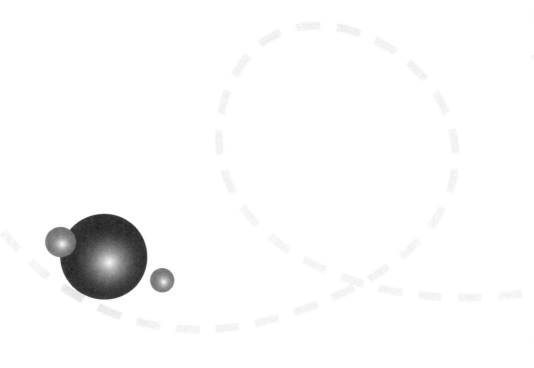

Water Wonder

Bring a pan of water outdoors and let your toddler explore its wonders through simple play. Encourage your child to experiment to see whether certain toys float or sink, which things tilt to their side or flip over, and what happens when ice cubes are placed in water.

Worm Crawl

Go outdoors at night and have your child act like a night crawler (an earthworm). How does a worm move? Have your toddler demonstrate. For extra fun, have your youngster attempt to wiggle and crawl around in a pillowcase or sleeping bag, with only her head and shoulders sticking out.

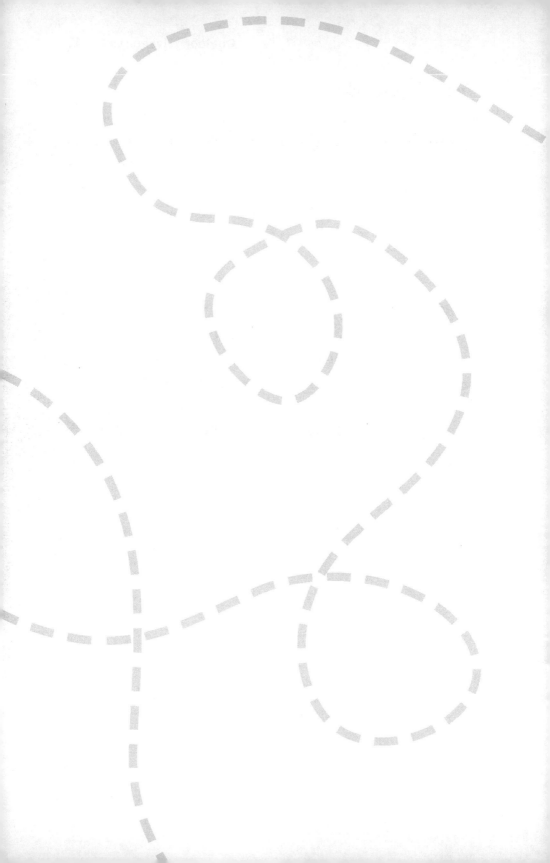

5

Toddlers on the Go

Keeping youngsters happy and entertained on road trips or airplane flights, whether on vacation or simply away from home and routine, requires planning and, in some cases, drastic measures.

American Flag Find

Many car dealerships and other companies display the American flag at their place of business. Turn spotting the displays into a counting game, with each sighting counting as one point until you get to 10. Kids get a bonus point for spotting state flags!

Animal Sound Game

This car game can be played with even the youngest of toddlers. All family members should be on the lookout for any animal. When one is spotted, the one seeing it makes the appropriate animal sound, and the rest of the family has to guess what it is. If everyone is on the ball, you could have a car full of moos or barks!

Apple Slice Snacks

Most kids like apples, but slicing apples on the road isn't practical, and who wants to eat brown-colored ones that don't look so fresh? A simple solution is to dip freshly cut apples in lemon-lime soda so that they retain their natural color. Have toddlers dip them and place them in plastic bags, and they'll be asking for those apple snacks in no time!

Backseat Driver

Create a steering wheel for your toddler to "help" you drive. A soft foam tube with the ends hot-glued together works well. To drive away boredom on the road, ask him to follow the road and make turns accordingly. If you're planning a long car drive, you can have your youngster decorate his steering wheel in advance so it's ready for action!

Bandage Puppets

Whoever would have thought a box of bandages could be so fun and entertaining? Many bandage boxes feature a variety of characters and designs. Buy inexpensive, theme-inspired bandages that have your toddler's favorite character, and show him how to place bandages on the ends of fingertips to provide instant finger puppets. Your toddler will have as much fun opening and applying the bandages as he will playing with them as finger puppet characters!

Barnyard Chat

Pretend you are in a barnyard and everyone is an animal. The only way you can communicate is with moos, meows, barks, or baas! It will make the trip go by quickly, and it's a fun way to reinforce animal sounds too.

Behavior Bucks

Create some simple "behavior bucks" to use as rewards for good behavior in the car and while on a trip. These bucks can be as simple as small strips of colored paper with a denomination on them or even just a smiley face. Reward kids for good behavior by giving them bucks that they can later redeem for a special treat or souvenir. Provide each child with a resealable bag (with his or her name on it), fanny pack, wallet, or some other holder to help them keep track of their "money."

Book Recording

Make a tape of yourself reading your toddler's favorite books and let her listen to them on the road while looking at the book. She'll love flipping through the pages and hearing your voice at the same time!

Car Fitness Fun

You can't do aerobics in the car, but kids (and adults) can do some simple exercises while on the road for fitness, fun, and to help prevent a case of the wiggles. Try some simple arm stretches or pointing and flexing toes while at stop signs, tightening arms and chest, clenching fists, and pretending to turn a steering wheel back and forth for five seconds and then releasing. Show your toddler how to lock fingers behind the neck and perform mini crunches to work on abdominal strength anytime there is a lull in activity while on the road or at the airport.

Color Contest

Name a color and have your toddler name as many of the things in the room that color as he can. Change colors and repeat the game. Keep changing colors for as long as there is an interest, and see which color "wins" the contest!

Color Find

Give your toddler a lap desk, washable markers, and a paper-filled notebook or dry-erase board. Have him draw things he sees of a certain color, using that color. Then see whether you can guess what he drew. For extra fun, take turns with who draws and who guesses the object!

Compass Commander

Let your kid become the commander with a compass. Even young toddlers will be fascinated with the different directions of travel. Youngsters can quickly learn how to read the four directions and then will have fun telling everyone which way the family is headed as you walk or drive.

Cookie Sheet Magnets

For some quiet and simple fun, pick up some inexpensive alphabet and shape magnets (usually available at dollar stores) for your road trip. Place the magnets on a cookie sheet for your child to move and rearrange. Bring along a plastic bag to hold extra magnet pieces not being used.

Count Down

Instead of counting up, count down! Have a countdown of objects to pass time and to encourage kids to count backward. Young toddlers may only be able to count from three down to one; older kids may count from 10 down to zero. Count blue cars, billboards, suitcases, whatever is in abundant supply.

Counting Items

Miles can disappear quickly when kids are focused on counting. Set a time limit, and together determine what you will count (for example, "Let's count the number of blue cars we see"). This encourages counting and observation!

Cow Counters

If you're in the country, count cows; if not, consider counting something that can be seen fairly regularly but not all the time. Or change up the item every time the number 10 is reached to keep the game more interesting.

Funny Watch

Be on the lookout for things that are funny! Laughter helps pass the time, and toddlers think all sorts of things are absolutely hilarious! See who can find 10 funny things the fastest (with detailed descriptions of WHY they're funny, of course!).

Glow Lights

If you and your child are traveling while it's dark, but it's too early for sleep, let her pass the time with glow lights. These inexpensive lights, which often last for hours, come in the form of sticks, necklaces, bracelets, and even creature figurines. Just make sure that the glow light doesn't interfere with or distract the driver.

Grab-bag Surprises

Planning a long road trip? Purchase some inexpensive treats and small toys for your youngsters ahead of time and gift wrap them. Provide each child with her own goodie bag, but with set rules that the contents can't be opened yet. Bring along a timer or alarm, and set it for whatever time you think is reasonable (45 minutes or 1 hour is ideal). One rule could be if kids mind you and don't ask the dreaded question "Are we there yet?," they get to pull out a wrapped surprise when the timer goes off. To pique their interest at the start of the trip, leave a small item in their seat that they get to open when you first get on the road.

I'm Thinking of a Color

Name a color and take turns with your toddler naming things that are that color. See how many you can think of (e.g., green is for grass, green beans, peas, frogs, grasshoppers, etc.).

I-spy

Even little ones can enjoy a simple game of I-spy (where the person who is "it" spots an object and others guess what it is) on the road. Keep it simple and more interesting by adding a quantity to find (e.g., "I spy 3 blue cars"). Once this is achieved, your child can have fun thinking of something for you to find!

Letter Hunt

Passing time in an airport or waiting without much to do? Have an alphabet search. Can your toddler find something that begins with the letter A? Even better, take turns so that everyone finds one thing starting with a letter and then all progress to the next. For very young toddlers, help them with the game by sounding out the letter and offering suggestions of things you see that start with that letter. This is a fun way to begin teaching alphabet sounds!

Me and My Buddy Vacation Memories

Your youngster can create her own special memory scrapbook from a family vacation or special trip. Before the trip begins, have your child pick one favorite toy or stuffed animal that will serve as her buddy on the journey. Using either a digital camera (preferred because you can easily delete bad photos) or an inexpensive 35mm camera, let your toddler set up a photo opportunity at stops throughout the journey. If your toddler is very young, take a photo of the child and her friend along the way. Kids aged 4 and older, however, can successfully use a camera to take their own photos. Let them take several on their own (it's really okay if they take photos at strange angles or extremely up close), and then be sure to capture a shot featuring them and a buddy at each stop. Later, assemble a scrapbook and let your toddler share her memories with friends.

Miniature Car Trip

Surprise your toddler with a new miniature car and let him use it to mimic the route you're taking. When the family car turns, have your youngster turn his car too. Encourage him to start and stop along with traffic lights and patterns.

Neck and Shoulder Rolls

When your child gets restless, show him how to do simple neck and shoulder rolls. Close your eyes and then roll your head around slowly, back and forth. Next, roll shoulders backward, and then forward. If space allows, extend arms straight and stretch out to the sides and then up toward the sky. Repeat.

Once upon a Time

Start a story with your child that begins with the words "Once upon a time." Create an interesting story based on characters that your child loves (princesses, pirates, bugs, etc.). Then stop and have your toddler determine what happens next. Pick it up from where she leaves off to create a zany adventure together.

Party Favor Fun

Save items your child receives in birthday party treat bags and dole them out when your child is taking a trip. The items are usually small and inexpensive, so it's not a big deal if they get lost or broken. Kids will have new things to look at and play with, and their small sizes are compatible with fold-down trays on airplanes and in cars.

Person, Place, or Thing

With simple explanation and coaching, you can teach your toddler the differences between a person, place, or thing. Turn it into a fun game that passes the time away. The one thinking of something has to designate which category it falls under, and the other player asks simple questions to help her determine what it is. Youngsters love thinking of something and seeing if you can figure out the mystery!

Pet Shop

Have your toddler pretend to be an animal in a pet shop just begging to get a new home. What does the animal do to get your attention? Does she bark or whine? Playfully swat at you? Purr? How does she act when you stop to take a closer look? Kids love to pretend to be animals, and the challenge will be to convince you to choose them and earn a new home. This is an easy pretending activity that can be acted out almost anywhere, including the car!

Picture Creation

Draw a picture and have your toddler make up a story about it. Afterward, let your child draw the picture, and you can make up the story.

Rhyming Games

A great preschool activity that helps prepare older toddlers for kindergarten is the rhyming game. This is a great on-the-go game that teaches the concept of rhyming. No supplies are needed, and it can be done in bursts to accommodate short attention spans. Start with very simple one-syllable words and help your toddler get started by listing three words that rhyme and then having him choose one more. Begin, for example, with "car, bar, far," and have him answer. Don't worry about whether he comes up with a real word or a made-up nonsense word. As kids get the concept down, you can change the number of words and the difficulty.

Road Race

Take turns choosing an item to spot from the car and count it as you see it (only up to a certain number, of course). It can be as silly as finding cars with antenna balls or bumper stickers. Whoever reaches the limit first gets to pick the object for the next round.

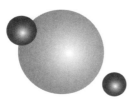

Shopping Buddy

Instead of dreading taking toddlers with you to a store, ask them to help out! The time it takes you to prepare beforehand will save you lots of effort while you're there. Make a list of items your toddler will be responsible for. (If you have time, draw the items needed next to the word or clip pictures of them from coupons or a magazine.) Explain how you need him to shop for the items on his list and that you will shop for items on yours. Stress that no items will be purchased that are not on the list. Ask your child what one thing (food item) he wants personally to be added to the list and indicate that there will be no more extras. When you arrive at the store, let your youngster navigate a separate kid-size cart (if he is able and the carts are available). Letting your toddler be "in charge" and take responsibility for some items will minimize the "I wants."

Sightings Report

Create a notebook with simple illustrations or magazine cutouts of items to be spotted and checked off while on the road. For example, one page can have 10 pictures of stop signs; your toddler will make an X through each one as she sees it. When all the objects in the notebook are sighted, give your child a small treat. This will really tick the time away!

Sign Shape Game

Road signs come in all sorts of shapes and sizes, so why not turn looking at them into a game? Youngsters can learn shapes easily by watching for signs. Parents can help by drawing and coloring basic signs and shapes on a piece of paper for youngsters to reference.

Signal Light Watch

Help beat boredom on car trips by playing the red light, green light game. Ask your toddler to watch the signal light at intersections and tell you its current color and what it is when it changes. If you have more than one child, make it a friendly contest!

Stargazing

For nighttime travel, have kids make simple telescopes out of toilet paper roll tubes decorated with glow-in-the-dark crayons, stickers, or markers. Have them peer out the window and look at the stars.

Stopwatch Countdown

Many inexpensive watches have stopwatch features that toddlers can successfully start and stop. Have them determine how long it takes to get from one town to another, or how much time goes by from the time you board the airplane until takeoff. While kids may not actually be able to tell time, they'll have fun with the concept of tracking time.

Stories on the Go

Have one person start a funny or silly story, then let someone else continue for a new round of adventures. After the story concludes have everyone draw a picture of their favorite scene. To keep participants interested in the game, use a simple 3-minute egg timer or a stopwatch and set a time limit for each round.

Story Creation

Ask your child to pick three things (for example, a princess, a dragon, and the ocean). Begin a story, then stop and have your child imagine what happens next. Take turns going back and forth, imagining an adventure!

Three of a Kind

Name a letter and have your toddler think of three things that begin with that letter. Then let her pick the next letter for you to name three objects.

Traffic Light Stickers

Use red, green, and yellow stickers and let kids record the different traffic lights you encounter. Create a simple graph ahead of time and explain that your child should place a sticker in the appropriate column every time a traffic light is encountered. (Consider using wax paper as an easy way to reuse stickers.) Youngsters will be so busy with peeling off the stickers, watching for traffic lights, and placing them in the right place that time will just zoom by. For older toddlers, add other stickers for items they might see along the way, such as animals, trucks, or weather.

Why Game

Kids love to ask questions, so why not make a game out of it? Take turns asking "why" questions and providing silly or serious answers. Encourage "thinking" questions, such as, "Why does a dog wag its tail?" You'll be charmed by your toddler's unique responses.

Family Fun

There's no shortage of
family fun when imagination,
activity, and role-playing are
added to the mix.

A Day at the Races

Set up some challenging jumps and races for those small cars that every household with young kids never seems to be without. Have your toddler set the course, complete with a starting line and a finish line. There's no need to assemble fancy racetracks when cars can careen over couches and slip under doorways or around corners.

Animal Safari Adventure

Imagination and role-playing are two huge favorites with toddlers, so a pretend safari adventure is sure to be a hit! Familiarize your toddler with animals that might be seen on a safari by reading an age-appropriate book or looking at a magazine or Web site that features these animals. Next, begin "packing" for the safari adventure by gathering up items you'll need along the way. Find safari-related stuffed animals that can be used for the journey or to foster imaginations (a cat can become a cheetah, for example). Place those throughout the safari area. Don your hats and sunglasses and off you go!

Talk with toddlers as you creep through imaginary foliage, look through binoculars (fingers) for "animal sightings," and walk quietly to avoid startling the animals. Do you hear the birds? See the monkeys swinging above? Can your toddler copy those noises? As you approach the watering hole, do you see how the elephants are using their trunks to cool off? Or hippos enjoying an afternoon swim? Uh oh! You've been spotted by a pride of lions! Maybe you'd better run back to the campsite and to safety! Afterward, color pictures of animals together, snack on bananas or other fruit, and watch an animal-themed movie together!

Any Reason for a Party Party

Create family fun with a party for any reason! Celebrate your toddler learning a forward roll at gym class, mom trying a recipe that the entire family loves, or dad volunteering to help coach T-ball. Whatever the reason, it's a fun way to celebrate as a family. Make a batch of brownies or a special treat and announce the celebration as a family. It makes ordinary events become more special!

Avocado Seed Planting

Save avocado seeds and have your toddler help plant them and observe them grow. Have each member of the family grow one and then observe their differences.

Awards Program

Create personalized silly awards for each member of the family. Print or draw awards on plain 8½-inch by 11-inch paper and have your toddler decorate around the wording. Ideas can include fastest cookie eater, most jumps on the bed, or silliest sounds!

Awareness Ribbons

Pick a cause that your family supports and together create some awareness ribbons for neighbors, friends, or classmates. Discuss how different ribbons represent different causes, and why wearing a ribbon shows you care. Be sure to use safety pins to fasten the ribbons on youngsters' clothes!

Backyard Picnic

What's not to love about an impromptu backyard picnic? Pack up picnic foods, tablecloth or blanket, and bug spray, and have a family picnic in your backyard. Bring some books, sunglasses, and sunscreen, and plan to stay awhile.

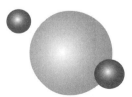

Brushing Teeth Time

It may sound silly, but start a tradition of brushing your teeth as a family for better hygiene and more together time! Kids who see mom and dad brushing their teeth will be inspired to do their best job, too. Place toothbrushes in a family holder and let your toddler put her toothpaste next to the adults' tubes. Everyone can prepare and then on "ready, set, go" brush their teeth while being silly or even dancing teeth-brushing jigs. Since everyone will do it together (as schedules permit), it also eliminates the "I forgot" excuses!

Soft Light Dinner

A softly lit dinner isn't just for romantics. Plan a simple dinner by soft lighting with your youngster, complete with formal silverware, tablecloth (this can even be a towel over a card table), and soft music. If your child likes pizza, make it a pizzeria night.

Caped Crusaders

Your family can become the next set of caped crusaders ready for the next big adventure! Create capes out of sheets or towels and establish a secret family code name and special superhero names. Each family member should also adopt a superhero power, such as becoming invisible, having super strength, or seeing through walls. Think up a special handshake, so you'll always know each other regardless of your assumed identities!

Character Charades

Play charades starring characters from your child's favorite movie!

Clothespin Fishing Game

When real fishing isn't practical, take your youngster clothespin fishing. Create some simple paper fish (and perhaps illustrations of silly things like an old shoe or a tire) and tuck them away where your toddler won't see them. Next, make fishing poles out of a stick and string and attach a clothespin or clip to the end of each. Show him how to cast the line over a couch, table, or even through a box (call it a pier), then clip on the different items to be "reeled" in. Consider making one catch extra-special for a fun treat!

Cookie Thank-you Send-off

Have your toddler help with baking cookies or other treats and mail them to U.S. troops as a thank-you for their service. This can be done around Thanksgiving or any time throughout the year!

Cricket Contest

Crickets are known to jump as far as two feet. Have a family cricket contest by marking off two feet and seeing if anyone can jump as far as these little insects.

Imaginary Cross-country Tour

If possible, invest in an inexpensive map of the United States. Place it on the floor and each week plan an imaginary driving adventure to one of the states. Kids love watching you look up facts and items of interest in books and on the Internet, so let them help you research some fun features and attractions of the particular state you are "visiting." Add to the fun by letting your child dress up for the trip (for example, by wearing cowboy boots when learning about a state known for cattle drives or rodeos). Reenact some of the highlights and help your child learn to pronounce the state's name. Let her trace the shape of the state and color it in. Family members can talk about states they have visited or where distant relatives live. Keep the interest alive by posting the map in a child's room and add something to each state after it has been "visited." Assign each family member a different color pushpin and place the pins in states where that family member has been.

Drumming to the Beat

Create a drum set using pots and pans and wooden spoons. Have one family member be the drummer, and that person picks the dancer. The dancer must dance while the drummer plays and then "freeze" when the drumming stops. Other family members serve as judges. If the dancer doesn't freeze when the drumming stops, he becomes the drummer and then picks a different family member to be the dancer.

If you prefer, all family members can participate as either drummers or dancers at the same time. This allows kids to produce some creative beats and focus on rhythm. Set out a variety of objects for the children to use as drums. Oatmeal boxes and coffee cans with plastic lids can serve as hand drums. For larger drums, place objects such as wastebaskets, ice cream buckets, and cardboard boxes upside down on the floor. Let the children experiment with the drums and talk about the different sounds they make. Which ones are best for making a sound like falling rain? Which ones are best for making the sound of elephants stomping? Tap out rhythms for the children to repeat. Play a variety of rhythm-based music and let the children accompany the music with the drums.

Family Campout

Plan a living room campout and involve your youngster in helping to decide on sleeping arrangements, packing requirements, food, and entertainment. Put up a small tent if you have one; if not, use some sheets and chairs to create your own tent indoors. All campers should pack an overnight bag for "roughing" it! Since it's a campout, no TV, radio, or phone calls are allowed. Pack a special dinner (brown-bag style) and make s'mores (graham crackers, chocolate bar, and marshmallow—not cooked over an open fire, of course) for dessert. Drink out of canteens or from drinks stored in a mini ice chest (there are no refrigerators on camping trips, after all).

As darkness approaches, turn all the lights down or off, turn on flashlights and lanterns, and have everyone gather around for some not-so-scary ghost stories. Show your kids how to make special shapes on the wall using flashlights and fingers. Then, just before one last trip to the latrine, read a good-night book by flashlight. The morning meal should also be something that doesn't need appliances for preparation (for example, eat cereal from the individual-size cereal boxes that open up to create bowls). Before returning "home" to a regular routine, the campsite needs to be packed up and everything put away—ready for the next adventure!

Family Celebrities

Take popular reality shows to a new level by adapting them for some fun family times that you'll all remember for a long time to come! Here are a few for starters:

Family Idol

Have your own Family Idol night, where family members perform their favorite songs to a live audience! Pick up a play microphone from a dollar store or toy store. (You can even make your own mike using a paper towel roll with a rag or soft item stuffed in at one end, or just grab a hairbrush.) Create a stage area and let your youngster dress up. Then play their song of choice in the background or let them perform a cappella! Family members can add to the mood by "introducing" the performer and pretending to be members of the press taking photos or video!

Dance-off!

Crank up a favorite kid tune and have a family dance-off! Have each participating family member create a move that everyone follows, and then switch to another!

That Kid's Got Talent!

Toddlers can do the most amazing things, so hold a weekly family talent show to showcase new skills! Kids can show how they've learned to fly like a bird, snort like a pig, wiggle like a worm, hop on one foot, and they might display a host of other talents that deserve cheers and recognition! Parents should get in the act by "learning" the skills from their youngster and even sharing a new trick or two themselves!

Family Masks

Have every member of the family make a mask and wear it for a specially created occasion or just for fun!

Materials
- paper plate
- scissors
- yarn, string, or elastic
- decorating items (paint, markers, crayons, feathers, sequins, etc.)
- glue, if needed

Cut a paper plate in half and then cut out holes for eyes, nose, and mouth. Punch a hole in each side and affix string on each end so it can be tied onto the head easily. Let family members decorate their own masks, and be sure to take a "masked" family photo!

Fitness Fun

A family that exercises together is apt to be healthier as a whole. Start an exercise regimen that is led by a different member of the family each week. Keep it simple and fun for everyone with jumping jacks, running in place, crunches, stretches, even a walk around the block or whatever works in your schedule. Liven it up by having your toddler choose family names for each exercise.

Folding Towels

Your toddler will feel very productive folding towels and washcloths for the family. Establish towel washing and folding as your child's special household chore, complete with gathering them from the laundry, placing them in the washing machine, moving them to the dryer, and then folding and putting them away. Be sure to let him know what a huge help it is, and maybe he'll keep doing it when he's older!

Hero Acts

On a weekend day allow your toddler to dress up as his favorite superhero and keep track of all the "heroic" things he does. Encourage your youngster to think of things he can do to make someone laugh or be happy, to help others, or to provide valuable assistance. Your superhero can open doors, help with groceries, sweep the porch, etc. Reward him with a favorite dinner or special activity.

In-home Movie Theater

Next time your family is settling in to watch a movie, why not make it a movie theater night at home? Have your toddler create movie tickets and determine what family members will want from the concession stand. Popcorn? Drinks? Some other type of treat? Let your youngster usher you to a seat and start the movie. You can even schedule stops for intermission and refreshments.

Mail Call

Who doesn't like getting mail (especially when it includes personal letters delivered right to your very own mailbox!)? Family members (this can be extended to neighbors or friends) should each create a personalized mailbox with a flag. Organize a mail station that includes blank note cards (3 by 5-inch work best), stickers for stamps, pens or markers, and anything else to use for letter writing. When a letter is left in the mailbox, the flag should be raised; when mail is retrieved, the flag should be lowered.

Parents can encourage basic writing by toddlers by leaving sample shapes, letters, and even names (for older toddlers to copy on paper and/or write). Drawings can be sent through the mail, too. Show youngsters how to affix a sticker on each letter as a stamp. To prevent toddlers from checking for mail every 10 minutes, set an official mail time each day (just like real mail delivery). Parents can write special notes of praise, give kudos for learning something new or trying a new food, or perhaps slip in a special package for something really special (success in potty training or giving up the pacifier, for example). Ask grandparents to get into the act, too, with an occasional special letter!

Materials
- shoe box or box of similar size
- decorating items of choice
- red construction paper or sheet of red foam to cut out flag shape
- clasp or brad (a type of flat nail) to affix the flag to the outside of the box
- 3 by 5-inch note cards
- stickers

Decorating choices can be as simple as covering the shoe box with comics from the Sunday newspaper, wrapping paper, or butcher paper that is adorned with a theme; decorating with feathers and sequins; or even using special designs that incorporate your child's favorite activities or characters. The top must be decorated or wrapped separately from the box so contents can be easily retrieved. A mail slot should then be cut into the top of each box by an adult, and the flag added on the side (use a brad so the flag can be raised and lowered easily).

Monkey See, Monkey Do

Undoubtedly you played this game as a child, but it's even more fun as a family. One member makes a funny movement or gesture, and others must try to imitate it. Take turns until all family members have had a chance to invent a move. For extra silliness, turn each of the moves or gestures into a silly dance sequence where each movement transitions into the next.

Movie Star Magic

Dress up your toddler and have him or her pretend to be a movie star. Jazz up a plain pair of sunglasses with rhinestones (girls) or select a dark pair (boys) and find "glamorous" clothes to wear. Daring duos can venture into a store with "star attitude" for extra fun. Show toddlers an exaggerated "it's all about me" walk.

Mystery Guest

Let your child have a "guest" (stuffed animal or special toy) at the table or on weekend outings. Having a guest encourages the building of communication skills. Since your child is speaking on behalf of the guest, adults can ask questions about the guest's name, interests, favorite foods, etc. Your child will have fun thinking of answers as to what his guest may like, and it encourages him to think about others and their needs.

No TV Day

What would your youngster do without TV for a day? Find out together! Announce No TV Day in advance to build anticipation. Talk about things you can do together instead of watching television. Plan a special game or craft, adventure outdoors, and make dinner together. Make it so special that your toddler will want to do it again! If you're lucky, it can become a weekly event (or even more frequent) and something you and your child will learn to treasure.

Pet Parade

Have your toddler and family pet (or stuffed animal) dress up with a theme and parade around the block or just the living room! Your child could be a pirate while the dog sports a fetching bandanna of his own, or the future rock stars could be paired with matching ankle bracelets. (Just be sure the four-legged family member is willing to participate!)

Photo of the Month

If you like to display photos in your home, choose a "family frame" that features a photo that is displayed and changed on a monthly basis. Make it a family decision to review and hang photos each month that signify family togetherness, achievement, or fun. Let your toddler help choose the photo of honor. Be sure to take lots of photos to give yourself several options.

Picnic Breakfast

Whoever said that picnics have to be lunch or dinner? Capitalize on mild outdoor weather and start a tradition of a picnic breakfast. Pack up fresh fruit, simple finger foods like donuts, or a single-serve cereal that can be eaten out of the box with a spoon and milk.

Picture Puzzle

Glue a photograph onto a cardboard back, and when dry, cut it into simple jigsaw puzzle shapes. Place the puzzle pieces into a resealable bag and have it available for kids to assemble for some afternoon fun! They'll delight in putting together puzzles of family members and pets!

Quality-time Shave

Next time daddy or grandpa shaves, let your toddler "shave" right alongside him using a cotton swab as a razor. Even better, give him (or her) whipped cream as his own pretend shaving cream. Toddlers will love putting some whipped cream into their hands, patting it onto their face, and then shaving it off with the safety of a cotton swab! This promises to be a photo opportunity!

Restaurant à la Home

Create some simple menus using photos from magazines. Let your child cut out and glue images onto paper that you can fold into a booklet; then have him decorate it with markers or crayons. Think of a fun name for the restaurant (e.g., Grayson's Grub House) and put the name on the menu cover. When mealtime approaches, have your youngster seat the family, pass out menus, and "take orders." Keep food choices simple so little hands can put the food items together on a plate and serve it. When finished, the wait staff should remove plates and put them in the kitchen. Dessert, anyone?

Role Call

How does a police officer act? Firefighter? Ballet dancer? Pop star? What about Spiderman? Make some flash cards using photos (or even stickers or drawings) of various characters and occupations. Have your youngster choose a card and then act it out. You have to figure out which one it is. Take turns acting out characters. Think of it as character charades!

Scene Stealers

Every once in a while before your child awakens, rearrange her toys or bedroom in a mischievous way, then have your toddler guess what is different. Be sure to let your youngster know that you are the one making the mischief, so there will be no concerns later on about monsters or nighttime visitors.

Scientific Survey

Get your toddler to try something new—in the name of science! Have her test out a new food item, game, or even item of clothing. First, show it to your youngster and let her look it over. Does she like the color? Feel? Shape? Why or why not? Does she think she'll like it? Why or why not? Now is the moment of truth: Have her try it and then see whether the predictions were correct. One fun example is tasting different flavors of jelly beans.

Seat Assignment Switch

Assigned seats at the table may work well most of the time, but why not change up the mix every now and then? Let your toddler assign seats for everyone on certain occasions, or make one chair the "honored family member" seat after a recent accomplishment or accolade.

Shoe Style Show

For whatever reason, kids just love trying on shoes! Have a shoe style show with your toddler by letting him try on all sorts of shoes, including those of dad and mom, older siblings, and even grandma or gramps! Clickity-clomping around in heels or yee-hawing in a pair of too-big boots is a blast. Just remember to teach toddlers that shoes must be returned to their proper location afterward or you'll have shoes all over your living room!

Sock-ball

Roll socks into balls and play catch indoors (with breakable items safely out of the way, of course!). Take a few outside and have a snowball-style fight!

Thumb Wrestling

Toddlers will love this easy-to-play game. Clasp hands by curving your fingers toward your palm and hooking them to your opponent's hand (which is hooked in the same way). Then do a count of "one-two-three" and see who can pin the other's thumb with his own. The best part is that it is a game that can be played quietly, requires no supplies, and keeps young ones entertained for a while, especially if they win at least some of the time!

Toddler Detective

It's a clue! Kids love playing detective, so outfit them with a notepad, magnifying glass, and detective clothes, and plan an age-appropriate mystery. Kids don't need to read to be detectives; the mystery can start with a ransom note for a missing toy and pictures that show clues for where to look next, all leading up to locating the wayward item along with a small reward for the sleuth! Turn it into a family activity by being a team of detectives (topcoats and hats optional!) and having everyone look for clues and solve mysteries.

Truth or Dare, Family Style

Make a game an occasional family tradition, and everyone may learn a few fun facts. Toddlers may need coaching to understand the premise at first, but soon they'll have fun asking mom or dad some silly questions or daring them to do something silly. Set up simple ground rules, including which subjects are off limits, and then have fun.

7

Parents' Night Out

When parents are away, the last thing they need to do is worry about their children's happiness and well-being, so planning easy and exciting activities for the sitter helps with the goodbyes.

Activity Paper Chain

Cut colorful paper strips and leave them for your child's caregiver along with a marker and stapler or glue. Have your toddler and the caregiver make a strip for each fun activity they did and then link the strips into a paper chain. When you return, your child can give you the chain of fun things done while you were away (such as going to the park, taking a walk, watching a special movie) and talk to you about each one. Display the chain in your toddler's room, and each time the babysitter watches your child, activities can be added to it.

All about Me!

Cut construction paper (or plain white paper) into fourths and staple it together to create a mini book. Write the title "All about Me" and include your child's name on the cover. What should be in it? Ask your toddler what she'd like to see featured. Suggest ideas about favorite foods and colors, what she does for fun, who her best friend is, what size clothes and shoes she wears, or why she is so amazing! You write in the responses. Have your youngster color the pages and draw a self-portrait (be sure to date it!). This makes a great "show and tell" item and a future family treasure.

Animal Zoo

Have your toddler create her own animal zoo scrapbook. Any type of animal can reside in your youngster's zoo. Collect several magazines or newspapers and leave a notebook and glue stick along with scissors for the caregiver. Have them identify and cut out animals together and add them to the zoo collection.

Balloon Ball

Blow up a balloon and bat it back and forth without letting it touch the ground. If this becomes too easy, blow up a second one for an extra challenge!

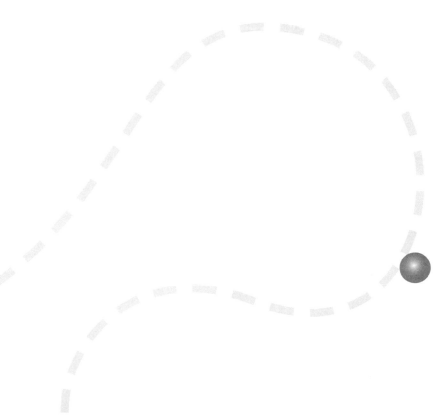

Buried Treasure Snack

Let your sitter create a special treat with low-fat vanilla yogurt or pudding (or a blue-colored variety). Stir in some gummy sharks and other critter shapes as available and have toddlers use their spoon to find and eat the buried treasure!

Cookie Decorating

When it comes to kids, decorating is the best part of making cookies! With that in mind, buy a roll of slice and bake cookie dough, a can of icing, and make sure you're stocked with sprinkles, candy bits, or whatever your kids love on cookies. Bake the cookies yourself ahead of time and have them cool and waiting. Set up the cookie-decorating station before the sitter arrives and make decorating part of the evening's fun.

Cup Hide

This is a simple game, but one that toddlers find fascinating. Take three small plastic cups turned upside down and hide an object underneath one of them. Move them around by sliding (not lifting) them and have your child try and pick which one has the item hidden underneath. If you like, make it a surprise game that becomes a special treat. Show your child how to do it and then have her practice on friends or family.

Dinner Party

Let your caregiver create a special occasion with your child by having a dinner party. While keeping the food itself simple and kid-friendly, encourage the meal to become a fancy occasion by sitting in the dining area, using special dishes, and dressing for the occasion. Kids can help serve (chicken nuggets on a platter can be fun). The sitter can choose mood music or other touches to make it a memorable occasion—without parents!

Egg Carton Ants

Create easy egg carton ants.

Materials
- cardboard egg carton
- pipe cleaners
- paint or markers
- scissors
- tape

Trim an empty cardboard egg carton ahead of time so that there are four 3-cup sections. Your youngsters can have fun helping their caregiver to create ants from the egg cartons. When turned upside down, the sections become the ant's body. An adult should poke three small holes on each side of the carton so that pipe cleaners can be inserted through to make legs (one pipe cleaner should form two legs, one on either side). Bend the pipe cleaners into leg shapes. Cut a pipe cleaner in half and stick it through two holes made at the top of the head to resemble antennae. Use tape, if necessary, to secure the pipe cleaner legs in place. The kids can color the ants or paint on eyes and decorate the body as desired.

Family Brags

It's not really bragging if you're reliving family history. Have grandma, grandpa, or a sitter talk about something really cool they can do. Let your toddler show off what he can do in reply. Your youngster may learn he can do something super-special (like touching his nose with his tongue or doing the splits!).

Family Tree

Grandparents can talk with their grandkids about genealogy—whose mom or dad they are and so forth. If possible, have some old family albums available for the grandparents and kids to look through as they talk about generations. Together they can create a family tree using photos or illustrations that can be proudly displayed in a child's room.

Famous Dads

Have a guessing game of famous dads. Even young toddlers will like hearing about who is considered the father of our country (George Washington), the creator of our world (God or whatever is in accordance with your personal beliefs), the fictional Father Time (a personification of time), and of course, the best father of all (their own!). Teach kids the concept of ancestors during the game. (Recognize, though, that they may not truly understand that grandpa is their dad's dad and that he was once a little boy, too.)

Footloose

Be footloose by removing shoes and playing patty-cake with your feet. Tots will love the opportunity to participate in this hand-game variation that ensures lots of giggles and foot-size comparisons. A variation is to wear silly socks and create silly feet characters to talk and interact with each other.

Fruit Punch Creations

Create your own "one-of-a-kind" fruit punch by mixing several flavors of juice. If your kids are normally juice drinkers, buy some different varieties and colors and tell your sitter to let the kids mix up their own specialty (with adult help, of course). Have special glasses for the drinks to be served in, with straws and fruit garnish for a special babysitter treat.

Generations Necklace

Create a "generations" necklace that kids will treasure. Use yarn and craft beads to create a necklace showing the generations of family members the child knows. Start with certain colored beads to represent great-grandparents, then string on grandparents, and so on. Have your toddler pick beads to represent himself and any siblings. Use a paint pen (available at most craft stores) to create dot designs or smiley faces on each bead. For extra bonding, grandparents should make a necklace at the same time and wear it along with the child for the rest of the day. Take a photo of everyone wearing the necklaces and frame it as a keepsake for your toddler.

Hand Jive Contest

Learn a hand jive pattern with a grandparent or sitter by taking the old "patty-cake, patty-cake" game one step further. Toddlers will delight in creating a hand-clapping, finger-waving, fist-popping move or in simply having a hand jive contest where you take turns creating silly gestures. This is a fun activity kids can do with someone who is not particularly mobile.

Hosiery People

Materials
- old pair of hosiery
- cotton balls or cotton batting
- yarn
- felt
- pipe cleaners
- scissors
- glue
- ribbon and other craft items
- decorating items

Invite your caregiver to make hosiery people (or creatures) by cutting out a section of stocking, knotting one end, turning it inside out, then stuffing it with cotton and knotting it closed. Let kids use the art supplies to create and glue on silly faces (use yarn for hair). Place one end of the "hosiery person" in a cup for easy stand-up and handling.

Job Jar

Create a job jar for your toddler and use each chore as a learning experience. Youngsters LOVE helping out, so why not teach them new skills while they're so eager? Consider simple tasks like matching socks, putting away dishes (if your child is capable), setting the table, sweeping, and folding washcloths. Let caregivers show your toddler a new task from the job jar. When all jobs in the jar have been tried, treat your child to a special family activity!

Laugh-off

Have a laugh-off. Who can be the funniest and laugh the loudest? It doesn't matter what you do—just be silly, goofy, and giggly together while having fun!

M&M Psychic

Put a single M&M in a small cup and have your youngster guess its color without seeing it. Give clues, with the reward being the M&M, of course! Kids love playing guessing games. You can also use other colorful treats, if desired.

Me and My Babysitter Journal

What parent wouldn't love to find out more about the fun activities their kids engage in with the babysitter? Many sitters are only too happy to do "extras" with the kids if given some encouragement (and the necessary supplies). Help sitters along by creating a simple journal made out of plain paper or construction paper, stapled together, and titled "Me and My Babysitter." When a sitter will be watching your li'l darling for several hours, ask her to create with your child a journal of the fun things they did during that time. Take a photo of the sitter and your child for the cover. If possible, create a babysitter idea box with some ideas of simple crafts or activities that can be easily accomplished. Not only does this set the expectation that their time together will include more than watching a movie; it also starts the creative juices flowing on what fun things they can create in the book together.

Mummy Wrap

Have your toddler use toilet paper to wrap up her caregiver as a mummy! They can design a fabulous outfit or even create a special head wrap for the occasion using only a roll of toilet paper and an active imagination. The giggles will assuredly abound!

Nature Queen or King

Materials
- poster board or foam paper
- dried beans
- glue
- scissors

Cut a strip of poster board or foam to fit around the child's head and then glue the ends together. While the glue is drying, go on a nature hunt to find items that can be glued on the crown (leaves, grass, wildflowers, etc.). The beans can be glued on as accents.

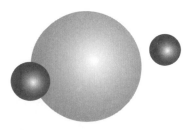

Paper Plate Dream Catcher

Have your toddler create a special dream catcher using a paper plate. This is a fun and simple craft that caregivers will enjoy making with your child.

Materials

- paper plate
- yarn of any color
- hole puncher
- beads and feathers (or any other decorating items)
- glitter glue
- curling ribbon
- stars (optional)
- scissors

Cut out the center of the paper plate (without cutting through the rim) so that you have between 2 and 3 inches as the outer band. Punch holes around the rim. Cut a long piece of yarn and pull it through one of the holes, knotting from behind. Let your child weave the yarn back and forth across the center opening and through the holes in a zigzag pattern, sliding a few beads through the yarn to be in the middle. Tie on new pieces of yarn when the end becomes short and keep zigzagging until a web is formed in the middle. Add 12-inch strips of curling ribbon by tying them through the bottom three holes. Glue or tie on to the ribbon some star accents, beads, and feathers, and then curl the remaining lengths of ribbon. Tie a length of yarn to two adjoining holes at the top to use as the loop to hang the dream catcher. Use the glitter glue as sparkly accents all around the plate. While making the craft, have a conversation about dreams and what good dreams your toddler has had and would like to "catch" and remember forever.

Plastic Bag Surprise

If your toddler attends a Mother's Day Out or other childcare program where you are apart, tuck a special surprise in her diaper bag or backpack. (Be sure to tell the provider about it and when it is appropriate to open the surprise.) The surprise can be as simple as a sticker, a small treat, a picture, or a note (for an adult to read to your child) that expresses your love. Keep the surprise very small and inexpensive; your youngster will look forward to seeing her surprise every time you're apart!

Popcorn Toss

Pop some popcorn (make extra to eat), and for some simple entertainment, put a bowl or cup a short distance away and play a game of popcorn toss. See how many kernels you can toss into the target. Add to the fun by moving the bowl closer or farther away and higher or lower.

Refrigerator Art

Caregivers can provide a pleasant surprise for parents by helping toddlers create a picture while mom and dad are out and displaying it on the refrigerator. Babysitters can bring along some washable markers, crayons, and paper just in case a supply is not available.

Role Reversal

When elderly grandparents watch an exuberant youngster, parents often worry that his sky-high energy levels and frequent demands may take a toll on even the most patient of grandmas and grandpas. One way to calm an energetic child is to play the game of role reversal. Tell the toddler he gets to "babysit Grandma" and explain all the things he gets to do while she is in "his care." Activities can include reading to Grandma, tucking her in for "quiet time," watching her favorite TV program together, and even getting her a snack, drink of water, and slippers. Toddlers like the notion of being in charge and will often act more calmly if they believe they are being put in a position of responsibility. While this game may not work for long periods of time, it can bring a grandparent some much needed downtime so they can reenergize in time for an afternoon walk or stroll to the park.

Shadow Hunt

Go on a shadow hunt indoors after dark to see which lights cast shadows and what neat shapes you can create. Keep it fun (not scary) by creating some funny finger creatures, and show toddlers how shadows can be really big or small, distorted or sharp.

Sort Smarts

Encourage your child's caregiver to play sorting games for fun and educational entertainment. Let your toddler sort different groups of items (separating books from fruit, for example). Older toddlers will be able to sort clothes coming from the dryer, help put away clean silverware from the dishwasher, and do other similar sorting activities.

Sunflower Retreat

Have grandparents plant some sunflower seeds in a large circle at their home (with their grandkids' help). The sunflowers will grow into a large hiding place and a safe play area. (If desired, corn or other tall plants can be planted for the same result.) When the growing season is over, save some sunflower seeds to plant the next year!

Teddy Bear Picnic

Have a teddy bear (or stuffed animal) picnic. This is a great activity with babysitters or older caregivers. Parents should put together a picnic basket of goodies (include Teddy Grahams and other animal-shaped snacks for extra fun) and drinks and have it ready to go. When it's time, youngsters collect the special guests who will join in the picnic. If weather permits, the party can go to the park, backyard, or patio. If not, an indoor picnic can be just as fun! Your toddler can introduce all her friends to her caregiver, and each of the guests can tell a little about themselves.

Theme Nights

Toddlers typically find any deviation from rules or set routines to be a riot, especially if it means Grandpa wears mismatched socks or the babysitter comes over with a shirt on backward. A great way to transition from parents to sitters (whether family member or paid babysitter) is to create a silly theme that all participants need to follow! And the best part is that toddlers usually think it's so much fun that they won't notice when you slip out the door! Ideas can include "hilarious hat day," "mustache mania" (yup, even Grandma needs to draw one on), or even "backward day" (this could include eating dessert first!). Just be sure to let the sitter in on the act in advance and secure his or her participation!

When I Grow Up

Using an inexpensive photo album or even a plain notebook, let your youngster create an album about what he'd like to do or be as a grown-up! This is a quiet activity that can be enjoyed with your child's sitter. Thumb through magazines or surf the Internet and cut out or print images of things your youngster wants to do when she grows up. Paste or tape them into an album, and let your toddler talk about all the possibilities while sharing it with others.

When I Was Little

Have grandparents, special family friends, or sitters play a game of "when I was little." Have your toddler start off by talking about a favorite activity he did when he "was little." Next, have the caregiver tell about beloved activities she did when she was young. Adults can introduce kids to things of days gone by. Kids, even young ones, like talking about things they did as babies and will enjoy it just as much.

Wish upon a Star

Create some simple paper stars on which to write down your child's special wishes (try to keep away from material wants). Tape them or hang them in your child's room, and before long, your child will be sleeping and playing under the stars of good wishes! A caregiver can start the project off by having a child create a few wishing stars and have them up in the child's room for a sweet surprise to parents later.

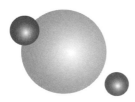

8

Special Events

Most kids love parties and special events, so here are some energy-management ideas to help with planning, countdowns, and celebrations.

Birthday Book

Create a story together of you and your child or your entire family as a special birthday celebration every year. Put the words down on paper and create a simple book that can be treasured and reread. Be sure to mark the date. You can make it even more memorable by having your toddler add a handprint and include a photo of himself with the book after it is completed.

Birthday Tree

On your child's next birthday, plant a birthday tree in her honor. Choose a quality shade tree that is well-suited to your area's climate. Help your child care for it as needed, and each year on her birthday, have a celebration by "her" tree. Take photos each year of your toddler next to the tree, place them in a treasured album, and marvel how both grow through the years!

Birthday Wish Countdown

How many times has your toddler asked you how soon his birthday is or how many days there are until his party? Here's a simple and fun way to help youngsters judge for themselves how long it is until their big day. Create this birthday countdown and your toddler can count for himself!

Materials
- handmade sign (decorate as desired) denoting event and/or date
- paper strips
- tape or stapler
- scissors
- decorating items (markers, stickers, etc.)

First, create a simple sign or birthday shape (cake with candles, the word "PARTY," or an appropriately themed picture). Then craft a linked paper chain with seven links for seven days. The links can be easily made by cutting 1 by 8-inch strips and then using a stapler or glue stick to form the link (remember to link them to each other in a row). If desired, your toddler can help decorate the links with markers or stickers. For each day of the countdown, let your toddler tear off a link first thing in the morning (or whenever it best works with the family schedule). When the links are gone and only the sign remains, then your toddler knows the BIG DAY has arrived!

Children's Book Week

This special week is celebrated every November. Celebrate with your child by checking out some new books from the library, purchasing a special book that interests your toddler, or reading the ones you already have. Then plan a special reading celebration time together to foster a love of reading.

Discovery Day

Celebrate Columbus Day in October by encouraging your toddler to act like an explorer and discover something new on his own.

The Eyes Have It!

September is Children's Eye Health and Safety Month, so combine some education with some kid fun! Take this time to teach kids about the importance of vision. Tie a blindfold on your child and have him experience what it's like not to be able to see. Fashion some simple glasses out of pipe cleaners and wear them around for a while as "glasses" to better relate to kids who wear them. Rub some petroleum jelly on a pair of your toddler's sunglasses and show him how some kids see (blurry) and why glasses or other aids help. Cover one eye with something like a pirate patch and ask if it affects vision. Explain the purpose of blinking and eyelashes.

Eyes Shut

Tie a blindfold on your toddler and have her practice feeling her way through a safe, clean room. Stay right next to her to avoid falls and hold her hand if necessary. This will be a fun game for the kids and may help those who have a fear of the dark.

Fairy Fun Day

Bring out some magical pixie dust (glitter) and take your child on an imaginary adventure to Fairy Land. With nothing more than imagination, toddlers can soar through the air and enter a wee world of fairies. Ask your youngster to imagine how big things must be from a fairy's perspective. Make a fairy wish, write it down, and record it in a special pixie-sized container.

Fire Safety Marshal

Assign your youngster the important job of serving as the family fire marshal. Have him "teach" all family members what to do in case of a fire, where the exits are, and what number to call in case of an emergency (9-1-1). Assign your toddler to conduct fire safety check-ups on a regular basis. Encourage a special family activity during Fire Prevention Week, which occurs in October each year.

Gift Clues

Turn the opening of presents into a fun time by having the gift giver provide a clue as to what the gift is and then letting everyone guess. This makes the opening of gifts a more engaging activity for everyone present.

Glitter Globe

Your youngster can create a beautiful glitter globe that is the right size for small hands.

Materials

- small jar (a baby food jar works best)
- beads and small plastic items of interest (hearts, stars, etc.)
- glitter (you pick the color)
- water
- mineral oil or glycerin (most pharmacies carry it) to cause glitter to fall slowly
- food coloring (blue can create an ocean, but you could use red and add plastic hearts or whatever color combination you want)
- craft glue

Add beads or other plastic items and glitter to the jar and then fill it with mineral oil or glycerin, water, and a food coloring of choice. How much mineral oil or glycerin you should add to water is somewhat subjective. It depends on how much glitter you prefer and how fast or slow you want the glitter to fall. If you use glycerin, start with just ½ teaspoon added to the water and see if you like the effect. You can always add more glycerin as desired. If you use mineral oil, start by using a 50/50 mix of oil and water. (You can experiment a little before sealing the lid.) Glue the lid shut. Kids love watching the glitter float and sparkle in their very own globe. This is a great craft to make at parties as a party favor.

Grandparents Day

This special day is celebrated every year on the first Sunday after Labor Day. Grandparents represent our heritage, and so often they provide babysitting assistance and heaps of love too. Have your toddler help to celebrate the occasion by making a special card for grandparents. It can be as simple as a traced handprint, a colored heart, or any free-form expression. Have your child sign his name as best as he can (you can print the name underneath, if necessary). If grandparents live far away, have your child call them. (What better way to learn the concept of talking on the phone?)

Handprint Stones

A handprint stone, whether mixed from prepared cement mix or from the ready-made kits that are sold at many craft stores, is sure to be a treasure and a favorite gift. Help your toddler push her hand into the mix, and then be sure to scratch her name and date alongside it. Consider adding stones, shells, or other keepsakes by pressing them into the concrete as well for a one-of-a-kind creation.

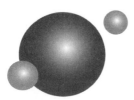

Healthy Teeth

February is Dental Health Month. Celebrate with your child by putting a positive emphasis on clean teeth! Let your child pick out a new toothbrush at the store and perhaps even a new "big kid" toothbrush holder and new toothpaste too. Find a book about teeth at the library or look up information on the computer about kids and their teeth. Have your child count his teeth. Cut out a tooth shape and have him decorate it. Make teeth brushing a family ritual. Read a story about the tooth fairy.

Kid's Day

We have Mother's Day, Father's Day, and even Grandparents Day, so why not proclaim a Kid's Day in your household? Establish a certain weekend day to honor your child and let your youngster make the key decisions on what fun activities to do as a family, including special meals. Create a crown proclaiming your toddler "King Kid" or "Queen Kid."

Make a Difference Day

This national day of helping others is celebrated on the fourth Saturday of October. Pick a project with your family, friends, neighbors, school, or church, and don't worry about how big or small it is: just make a positive difference. Even small toddlers can help clean up a local park (keep it age appropriate by giving youngsters tasks such as sweeping or other safe activities), visit with an elderly neighbor, donate clothes to a homeless shelter, or use some of your child's savings to purchase a new toy for a needy child.

Make Your Own Party Hats

Sure, you can purchase party hats, but toddlers will have twice as much fun making them as a party activity.

Materials
- colored construction paper (the bigger the paper, the bigger the hat)
- glue sticks
- decorating items such as glitter, beads, or stickers
- precut thin strips of colorful paper (recommended size is ½-inch by 8-inch) that are folded accordion-style for effect (for tassels at the top)
- hole puncher (or scissors)
- tape
- stapler (optional)
- yarn or string

Let kids choose their favorite color construction paper and decorate it as they choose with materials at hand. Then have them pick 6 of the accordion-folded paper strips. Lay the strips out on top of each other, fan out one end, and either staple or tape them together at the other end. Then, either staple or tape that to the middle of one of the long edges of the construction paper (on the undecorated side), with the crinkle strips extending outward. (They will become the ends that stick out at the pointy top of the hat.) Next, simply roll the paper (decorations on the outside) into a cone shape and glue, tape, or staple in place. Finally, punch a hole on either side of the hat and tie a 12-inch piece of yarn or string onto each end. (Kids prefer ties over the annoying elastic typically found on store-bought party hats.) Place on kids' heads and have your camera ready!

Mask-erade Party

Kids love masks and creating a mystical personality, so let them make a unique one in minutes for a party or a special occasion! The photos will be priceless.

Materials

- fun foam of various colors
- glitter glue
- feathers
- sequins
- beads
- markers
- other decorating items (use your imagination)
- scissors
- hole puncher (not required)
- yarn or string

Adults should precut a variety of basic mask designs (over the eyes only—like masks from the movie *The Incredibles*). Cut out eye holes, punch a hole in each end, and tie on string or yarn long enough to be tied together at the back of the child's head. This generally provides for a better fit than the stretchy elastic, which can pinch or get caught in hair. Turn the youngsters loose at the "mask creation table" and watch the fun. Provide some pictures of action heroes or masked ball selections to help generate ideas. Have toddlers participate in another activity while the masks dry (be careful that they don't overdo the glue and lengthen the drying time), and then have some masked crusader fun!

My Wish List Book

Whether their wishes are for Christmas, a birthday, or any other celebration, toddlers can create a "wish list" journal that they can carry around and show to others. Youngsters can draw, cut out and paste in pictures, or write about some of their wishes. (Remind them that not all wishes have to be for new toys or something purchased; wishes can be for snow, a new friend, or getting to eat the coveted turkey leg at the next big holiday meal!)

National and Global Youth Service Day

National and Global Youth Service Day, occurring in April of each year, is touted as the largest service event in the world. Activities are designed to help support youth on a lifelong path of service and civic engagement. Toddlers can join in by helping you with disaster relief drives, food banks, donating books for poverty-stricken areas, and more. By instilling service goals on this special day and throughout the year, you can help your toddler understand charity and service at a very early age.

National TV Turnoff Week

National TV Turnoff Week is held every April. In celebration of this event, how about letting your toddler create her very own TV show instead of simply watching cartoons or a video? Let the potential thespian in your child come out through some creative play. Start by helping her brainstorm a topic and the TV show's name, and then she can be the star! After all, who needs to watch television, when you can be the creator, producer, and lead actor of your very own? Keep it age-appropriate by letting the show be as simple as a dance performance or a song (for younger toddlers). Add fun by videotaping it and then having a special premiere.

9-1-1 Day

This special day happens every September, but you don't have to wait until then to teach your child about "9-1-1" and when this ever-important phone number should (or shouldn't) be dialed. Even very young toddlers can understand the notion of an emergency and what to do in certain critical situations. Post the number by the phone where your child can see it to recall the number in case the unthinkable should occur.

100th Day of the Year

Observe the 100th day of the calendar year (occurring every year on April 10 or 11) by having a surprise celebration for your child. It can be as simple as a plastic bag filled with 100 Cheerios or Froot Loops that become breakfast that morning, a present of 100 pennies or stickers, or even "I love you" written 100 times on a piece of paper. Make it an annual tradition that your child will cherish!

Read Across America

The National Education Association's Read Across America is a reading motivation and awareness program that calls for every child to celebrate reading on Dr. Seuss's birthday, March 2. Parents can celebrate the beloved author's birthday by sharing quality time with their child over a book. And whether it is a Dr. Seuss classic such as *Green Eggs and Ham* or a non-Seuss selection, this celebration will help parents and caregivers instill a love of reading in toddlers.

Stop, Drop, and Roll

Teach fire safety by playing a fun game with a serious message: show your toddler how to stop, drop, and roll in case clothing or hair catches on fire. Demonstrate safety measures with a blanket. Use the month of October to teach various fire safety measures, such as what to do, how to exit the house, and where to go in case of a fire.

Tickets, Anyone?

Create magic tickets for your child to receive for good behavior or deeds and then to redeem for an adventure. Have your toddler collect at least four tickets (you determine when and how they are given) and place the tickets in a special passbook. Once four tickets are earned, your child can then turn one back in for some family fun. Keeping a minimum number teaches basic counting skills and requires your toddler to think about choices.

Tissue Flowers

These tissue flowers make a great gift for Grandparents Day!

Materials

- 3–5 different colored sheets of tissue paper
- pipe cleaners
- vase (if desired)

Let your child choose three or four different colored sheets of tissue paper and set them on top of each other. Fold the stack of tissue papers accordion- or fan-fold style and wrap a pipe cleaner or twist tie in the middle of the folded tissue. Next, have your toddler carefully open his flower by pulling the different colors of paper either up or down as desired to separate and fluff the "petals." Add a pipe cleaner stem, and if desired, craft leaves from additional pipe cleaners.

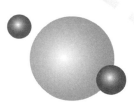

9

Calm and Quiet

Silence can be hard to maintain for little ones, but with proper planning, parents can encourage calm and quiet behavior for appropriate times. These activities are for just those times.

Animal Cracker Parade

Provide some animal crackers as a special treat and organize an animal cracker parade. While setting limits as to how many can be eaten, let your child have fun with the animal crackers by creating a parade, circus, or animal show. You can even encourage your child to name the animals he knows and sort the same animal crackers into groups.

Blindfold Draw

Have your toddler try to draw something while blindfolded. Choose something simple, such as a star, a car, or even a person, and tell your child step-by-step what parts to draw (wheels, legs, etc.). Between items, have your child put her pencil or crayon down and then pick it back up and try to resume drawing in the same spot while blindfolded for a more interesting outcome.

Chalkboard Fun

If you merely need your child to remain quiet and don't mind a little mess, have your toddler entertain herself with a mini chalkboard and some chalk. Don't forget the eraser, and be sure to have a damp washcloth handy for a quick wipe-down afterward.

Cheerios Fun

Give your toddler a pipe cleaner bent on the end and let him string Cheerios, Froot Loops, or any O-shaped cereal. (Of course, it's okay if he snacks on a little at the same time.) When the pipe cleaner is full, shape it into a bracelet. Encourage your child to get creative and make different jewelry items.

Family Photo Album

Plastic photo albums can be found for under a dollar at many stores. Pick one up, put your child's name on the front, and then tuck in some photos of the family, your home, or your pet. Label the photos on the front so that when your child shares his album with others they'll know what's in the picture. Allow your youngster to take his photo album to daycare or on family visits. During times when silence is golden (such as in church or at weddings), this will be a welcome item to keep your toddler busy. From time to time, add new photos featuring your star. Kids love showing off photos of key events and loved ones.

Felt Cutouts

Felt cutouts make a quiet and fun activity for toddlers. And, with felt pieces typically costing 20 cents or less at stores, it's easy to make several cutouts to entertain your child. Decide what interests your child and cut shapes reflecting that. Ideas include making a child's body and then having your toddler "dress" the boy or girl with clothing, hair, accessories, etc. You can also make rocket ships, animals, etc. The felt pieces can easily be stacked and then removed and reused. Store the cutouts in a plastic bag or small tote for easy carrying.

Finger Bugs

Whoever knew that pipe cleaners could be so entertaining? Bend a pipe cleaner in half and gently twist it onto your child's index finger. Shape both sides into simple wings, leaving the ends pointing out like antennae. Let your toddler quietly entertain herself with her bug friend.

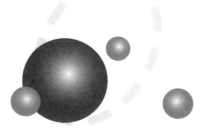

Good Behavior Goody Bags

Create a surprise goody bag for toddlers to keep them quietly entertained and happy at functions where kid sound effects are not part of the program (meetings, weddings, church services, etc.). For longer events, parents need to be especially creative, perhaps by crafting two or three different play items that will leave guests and hosts appreciative of how well behaved your toddlers are!

Parents need to be sure that toddlers won't screech when receiving a new item and that the packaging and items are not noisy when opened or played with (for example, don't place items in paper or plastic that kids can tear into, causing distracting noises). Tell them it's their "reward" for such wonderful behavior and then dole out small items to keep them quietly interested. A good example is to provide your child with a cotton or soft-material tote bag that is accessible and easily carried by little hands. Have a first treat inside and then, depending on the length of the program or service, be sure to refresh the bag with some additional attention-keepers throughout the function.

Sure-hit Items

- mini stuffed animals
- small plastic soldiers, pirates, or tiny dolls (but not the tiny shoes and clothes)
- travel-size notepad with washable crayons
- small pop-up or interactive books
- gummy candy in individual servings (these are not messy, and most kids can munch on them quietly)
- small toy cars (but not if your youngster likes to make loud sound effects and smash them into each other)
- bottle of water with an easy-to-open sports top
- plastic jewelry meant for children

The bottom line is, if it requires any type of batteries or features any type of sound effect, leave it at home!

Homemade Putty

Make some homemade putty in advance and then have it on hand for "quiet time."

Materials
- 2 parts white glue
- 1 part liquid starch
- small bowl
- airtight container

Mix the glue and starch in a bowl. Let it dry until the putty is workable. Add more glue or starch until the desired consistency is reached. Store in an airtight container.

Magnet Magic

Magnets are fascinating and quiet, and they usually keep little ones captivated for some time. (Be sure kids are old enough to understand that magnets should not be put in their mouths.) Many stores carry a variety of simple magnets, and presenting toddlers with a collection of a few in a plastic bag can keep them busy creating designs on a metal surface or figuring out the invisible force between them!

Mail Sorter

Teach your child about mail. Sorting mail by recipient is a great way to encourage name recognition and early sounds. Let your toddler's job be to open all junk mail addressed to Recipient or other mail that is clearly not important correspondence. Show her how to open mail so that the contents can be retrieved undamaged. Save the mail to be opened during times you need your child to be quiet and busy!

Mix Master

Create a grab bag of three distinctly different items, such as balls, beans, and jacks. Blindfold your toddler and see how fast she can sort the objects into different groups.

No-Speak I-spy

Play I-spy without speaking. Using only hand motions or glances, try to guess what object is being looked at.

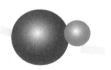

Peanut Butter Clay

(Not for kids with peanut allergies.) You can judge for yourself whether this meets your standards for table manners, but you really can make edible clay out of peanut butter! It's finger lickin' good!

Ingredients
- 1 cup smooth peanut butter
- ½ cup honey
- 2 cups nonfat dry milk

Mix together the peanut butter and honey. Add the dry milk a little at a time, kneading it in until the mixture feels soft and pliable. Kids can use other edible items such as raisins, chocolate chips, or sprinkles for decorations, if desired.

Pencil Creatures

Using either foam beads or clay, have toddlers create a creature to put on the end of a pencil. The pencil shape and length are great for allowing kids simple pretend play. This is a quiet activity that encourages creativity. For younger toddlers, use new, unsharpened pencils.

Pipe Cleaners

They bend, they twist, and they can make amazing things! They're pipe cleaners! Kids can create rings, flowers, balls, or whatever their imaginations can dream up and, best of all, they make no sound at all! Buy a bag of multicolored pipe cleaners and let kids play with them when complete silence is essential!

Popsicle Stick Puppets

Parents can assemble materials for a puppet-making craft for toddlers that will keep them quietly entertained. Cut out some basic shapes that best spark your toddler's interest (princesses, space rockets, silly monsters, etc.). Foam paper works well, but regular paper or construction paper can also do the job. A basic body can be crafted from the foam, along with various outfits (think simple shirts or hats) from which the toddler can choose. Use craft glue (or hot glue if the adult does the gluing) to affix paper or foam shapes to a Popsicle stick. Have a variety of sticks and cutouts on hand, and perhaps one finished Popsicle stick puppet that can serve as a guideline (or inspiration).

Quiet Sit

Have a contest to see who can sit quietly the longest. The last one to say something wins. Make it more fun by rewarding the winner with a small prize or treat, such as a piece of candy.

Raisin Brigade

Let your youngster transform raisins into soldiers or small characters for quiet playtime fun and a tasty snack. Celery can become a bridge; a carrot can be a tall building. Have your toddler line up and then count the raisins and have them disappear, one by one.

Rigatoni Necklace

Let youngsters string uncooked noodles on yarn to make a necklace, belt, or original noodle designs. Rigatoni is the preferred pasta for kid crafts because the large openings will fit over their small fingers and are easily managed by youngsters.

Rock, Paper, Scissors Game

Not only is this hand game fun and simple, but it also teaches toddlers about the concepts of weight, breakage, and covering an item with another. Plus, once they get the idea of the game, it's simple and fairly quiet entertainment that requires no preparation, no materials, and can be played anywhere! (Remember, paper covers rock; rock breaks scissors; scissors cut paper.)

Snake Plate

A paper plate, scissors, and crayons or markers are all that is required for this quiet craft. Cut a paper plate into a spiral, beginning at the rim. Keep the cut at least an inch wide. When the spiral is complete, it becomes a snake! Let your toddler color the snake and then make it quietly slither.

Stare-off

Who can outstare the other without cracking a smile or looking away? Silly faces are definitely allowed. To keep things quiet, add a "penalty" for laughing.

Statue Stare

This may be even tougher than the stare-off for a wiggly toddler! Pretend you are statues. The first person to move loses.

Strange Creatures

Fold a sheet of paper into thirds. On the top third of the page, one person draws or colors the head and neck of a person, object, or creature. Fold the paper back so that what was drawn is not visible and have the next person draw arms and a body. A third person then draws legs and feet without seeing the other pieces. Unfold the paper and have a look at your strange person or creature. The person who drew last becomes the first the next time until all have had a chance to draw the head.

Straw Adventures

Drinking straws, especially those with the bendable necks, can provide for some quiet fun. With a box of straws available, have your toddler imagine some "straw friends" and have them play with each other and go on an imaginary trip. What do the straw friends think when a person grabs them to use in a drink?

Tissue Surprises

When an event calls for a toddler to be quiet for an extended period of time, make some "quiet keepers" ahead of time. Place a small and noise-free trinket inside some tissues, then wrap it using a simple string or ribbon. The tissue will prevent a mess and can be opened quietly. Place a few in a tote and let your youngster open one periodically to discover a small car, fruit candy, doll, writing/drawing journal, or other quiet plaything.

Tongue Roll

Can your toddler touch his nose with his tongue? Roll it? See who can do something really silly without making a sound.

Tummy Jiggle

Are you stuck somewhere with nothing for your toddler to play with? Take turns making your tummies jiggle, toes wiggle, or eyes cross. Think of silly things you can do with your body without getting out of your seat or causing a disruption.

Whisper Words

How softly can you whisper? Pretend that whispering is the only way you and your toddler can speak; anything louder can't be heard. Shhh!

With Eyes Closed

With her eyes closed, have your toddler use only her sense of feel to determine what object you're holding or how many fingers you're holding up. Add other easy-to-grasp objects such as a blade of grass outside or a drinking straw for some quiet, simple fun.

Yarn Art

Give your child some yarn and encourage yarn art play for some quiet entertainment. Let him unwind some yarn, tie it around hands or fingers, and then roll it back into a small ball of yarn again. Tie a loop at one end to string over fingers for web creations. When done, simply store the yarn in a plastic bag to use another time.

10

Memorable Play Dates

Most toddlers are social creatures by nature, and play dates help build social skills and boost self-confidence.

Beanbags

Place beans in snack-sized plastic bags and seal them to create beanbags. Line up an empty box or wastepaper basket and create a bean toss. Whoever gets the most beanbags into the box in a single turn (using five beanbags is a good number) wins the game!

Blanket Toss

Have kids gather around a large blanket or throw. (For only two kids, use a towel.) Place a lightweight ball in the middle and have them bounce it as high as they can without it bouncing off the blanket. An alternative is to use two or three smaller balls for a greater challenge and even more fun!

Blindfold Taste Test

Have toddlers "taste test" different drinks or snacks while blindfolded. With a little imagination, you can make it creepy for Halloween by having them eat worms (gummies) or drink witches' brew (juice), or you can give it a holiday theme such as "love lemonade" or "kiss juice" for Valentine's Day. It can even be as simple as seeing whether "red punch" or "blue punch" rules the playgroup! The food and drink that win will be the choice of snack for the next get-together.

Book Exchange

Parents with multiple kids often find that they have heaps of books around the house. Why not make your next playgroup a book exchange? Have each child bring four gently used books that they won't mind parting with (no torn or missing pages) and lay them all out for display. Have each child pick a "new" book from the selection (start with youngest kids) and then repeat until all kids have four books to take home!

Breakfast of Champions

Youngsters can help you make breakfast by laying out canned cinnamon rolls before you bake them, cracking eggs and helping to scramble them, and pouring milk, for example. Make it their job to help with a meal each week to build confidence and encourage independence in the kitchen later on. For a special playgroup outing, invite a couple of friends over and let them all create their very own special breakfast. (Extra adult helping hands are strongly recommended for this one!)

Buried Treasure Hunt

Have kids come to the next playgroup dressed like buc-
caneers ready to dig for buried treasure. Bury play jewelry, plastic gold coins, gemstones, and other pirate
booty in a large tub of sand or sandbox. Give each child
a bucket and plastic shovel, and use sieves to sift
through the sand. Bury enough so each lad and lassie
gets plenty of treasure!

Color Clap

Have toddlers sit in a circle and have an adult lead the
game. When a color is named, kids clap, but they can't
clap on any other word. For example, say "mean-jeans-
GREEN-shoe-two-do-BLUE." Rather than eliminating
players when mistakes are made, keep it noncompetitive by having the child run around the circle and then
sit back down.

Chocolate Dipping Party

The next time the playgroup gets together, have a dipping party. Melt chocolate and let toddlers dip and decorate food items such as sliced apples and large marshmallows.

Ingredients
- melted semisweet chocolate chips (using a double boiler over medium heat)
- sprinkles
- nonpareil candies or other edible decorating items as desired.

To avoid burns, pour melted chocolate in small bowls for each child after it has cooled to a reasonable temperature. This will also eliminate community double-dipping and "sharing" issues. Kids can then dunk their chocolate-dipped food into the decorating goodies. Let treats cool and harden for 20–30 minutes. Enjoy!

Coloring Book Exchange

Create a monthly coloring book exchange with friends, neighbors, or kids at daycare. Have every parent bring un-colored coloring book pages (1 per participating child) and then have a page exchange. (Bring 10 pages if 10 kids are participating, for example.) This is a more fun and affordable way to get kids a wide variety of themed pages to color. Tots will have a broad selection of action heroes, princesses, animals, and beloved characters to choose from. A parent can then staple the pages together with a blank sheet on top as the book's cover for a unique coloring book all each child's own.

Dancing with Stars

Have a toddler dance-off on the next play date. Start some kid-friendly, energetic music and let the kids go at it! After the song is over, pair them off and have them do any type of couple's dance (where they copy each other, dance together, or simply dance side to side or back to back in pairs). End the dance party with an easy line dance (it can be as simple as the classic Hokey Pokey).

Duck Duck Goose with a Twist

Play the ever-popular duck-duck-goose game with a twist. (Duck Duck Goose is played with kids sitting in a circle and the person who is "it" tapping other kids on the head one at a time saying "duck" until one is selected to be the goose. The one who is "it" then yells "goose!" and the selected child chases the other back around the circle to try to catch him before he sits down in the spot where she was originally sitting before she was picked. The one left standing becomes "it.") Vary this kid favorite by having whoever is "it" create a different chant, such as "Dog Dog Cat" or "Star Star Rocket." Kids will have as much fun thinking up new combinations as they will playing the game!

Fashion Show

If your toddler has a special sense of clothing style or just likes to play dress-up, organize a toddler-friendly fashion show. Kids can choose costumes to model and then prance about and show off their attire to willing watchers. Add music, create a "runway" (as simple as an open path area), and then finish with hearty applause, photographs, and refreshments!

Food Play

Who needs a boring old sandwich when you can create a meal with lots of personality? Begin by making a sandwich (or other meal item) in a funny shape. Have bowls of food items such as shredded carrots, lettuce strips, grapes, raisins, or pretzel sticks that can be used and shared among toddler friends. Have a contest to see who can create the funniest edible item using the food choices provided. Kids will find it amusing that they actually have approval to play with their food and will find this activity wildly entertaining!

Fossil Find

Using air-drying clay or Play-Doh, press imprints of small bones, shells, bugs, or other interesting bits of nature to make a mold. Let the molds dry and hide them around the house or yard; then let kids go on a fossil find.

Fruit Pizza

Instead of standard junk-food fare at your next get-together, how about having kids create their very own fruit pizza? First, prebake a sugar-cookie crust. (The easiest way is to roll out prepackaged sugar-cookie dough.) Then press the dough into a pizza pan and bake according to directions. Let toddlers spread a thin layer of white icing (or cream cheese with some sugar or sweetener added) and decorate the pizza with fruit such as sliced grapes, kiwis, strawberries, blueberries, peaches, bananas, or whatever their favorite is! Cut the fruit pizza into slices for a tasty treat!

Guess How Many

Toddlers love guessing games, and this one involves a simple prize that will surely be a hit. Fill a clear glass jar with any type of candy or small toys and let kids all have a chance at guessing how many items are inside. The closest guess wins, and that child gets the first pick of any prize in the jar. Everyone else gets to choose something after the winner. This game works with party favors, too. Place different items in the same jar and allow each child to guess how many of that kind are inside to win. (It's helpful to narrow the guessing range by saying it is between "10 and 25," for example.)

Hot Potato

This classic childhood game can be played with a beanbag, small ball, stuffed animal, or—you guessed it—even a potato! Play music while the kids sit or stand in a circle and pass the potato around like it is hot! hot! hot! When the music stops, the child left holding the potato is out. (Or you can avoid the "out pouts" by having the child do something silly.) When no music is available, have someone turn his back to participants and count to 20.

Luau Luncheon

Play dates make for simple enjoyment at a neighbor-hood park or playground, inside a host's home, or at a kid-friendly restaurant. Sometimes, however, it's fun to create a themed lunch to celebrate a special occasion or just to do something extra fun for the kids. A luau luncheon is sure to be a crowd-pleaser, and the best part is that it is inexpensive to do and simple to plan!

Ask participants to show up dressed in Hawaiian-themed attire. There's no need to purchase elaborate outfits; a flower in the hair, Board shorts, or flip-flops is perfect. You can even go a step further and pick up plastic leis or grass skirts for the kids to wear. Hawaiian music can set the tone if anyone has tunes available.

Provide each guest with special "Hawaiian" (fruit) juice and serve appetizers consisting of grapes, oranges, melon, and cubed cheese; grilled chicken with slices of pineapple (picky toddlers can always leave the pineap-ple on the plate) and slices of Hawaiian sweet bread for the main course; and flower-themed cookies for dessert. Have kids play simple games like limbo or hula hoop, learn a basic hula dance (anyone can create a few basic moves and hand motions), and end the party with a performance!

Mock Slumber Party

Most toddlers are too young for slumber parties but would surely love getting invited to an evening event. A recommended party time is 5–8 PM. Kids should come dressed in their pajamas and bring a favorite stuffed animal, sleeping bag, and pillow. Entertainment can include a twilight walk, movie night with popcorn while tucked in their sleeping bags and propped on their pillows, and story time. When their parents pick them up, they'll be all ready to put to bed!

Orange Juice Pops

Make a simple and tasty toddler treat for when friends come over. Freeze orange juice in plastic ice-cube trays (stick a Popsicle stick in each cube when the mixture becomes semi-frozen). When toddlers clamor for a snack, serve up orange juice pops that are healthy and tasty!

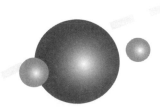

Paper-bag Puppets

Making puppets out of paper bags is easy to do and fun for toddlers. Have kids use glue, colored-paper scraps, pipe cleaners, markers, or whatever you find to give their puppets the identities they desire! For added durability, cover the paper bag with construction paper folded to conform to the folds of the bag. This is a simple craft to make with youngsters and can also be done with a particular theme or holiday.

Penny Pleasure

Encourage toddlers in a playgroup to collect and save pennies all year long, beginning at New Year's if possible. As the end of the year draws near, pool the money, count the coins and convert them to paper money at a bank, and then use the money to donate items to kids in need or to another agreed-to cause. Let all the youngsters sign a card (or use handprints if too young) to attach to the gift.

Pin the Tail on the Donkey Variation

Who needs to stick with traditional Pin the Tail on the Donkey when the alternatives are endless? For this variation, choose something your child is crazy about and make a game using poster board and a little creativity! Draw your child's favorite object or character (pirate, princess, race car, etc.). Give each toddler in the playgroup a crayon, blindfold them, and have them draw on the eye patch, crown, or tires, etc., as appropriate. It's cheap, safe, and quite honestly more fun!

Pixy Stix Candy Art

Have your toddler make layered art using Pixy Stix candy instead of sand. This powdery candy comes in a variety of colors and flavors, which you can let your youngster layer into a transparent container like sand art. As long as you watch your child's consumption, it makes for a fun—and yummy—craft!

Prize Box

With music playing, have the children sit in a circle and pass around a box without looking inside. When the music stops, whoever is holding the box gets to open it and keep the prize inside. That child then leaves the circle and the game continues with a new prize inside the box. (It is usually best to have all the prizes be of about the same value.) Eventually, all the toddlers will have won a prize.

Cotton Swab Painting

Supply plain paper and use cotton swabs dipped in watercolor or other washable paint to let toddlers paint pretty pictures without a lot of mess.

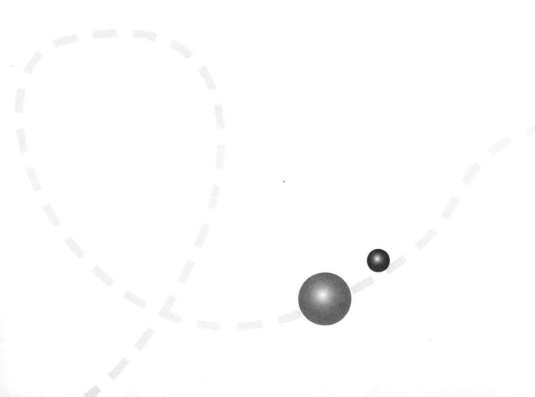

Sand Art, Homemade Style

Instead of purchasing pricey colored sand or sand-art kits, make your own. Add a few drops of food coloring to clean, dry sand in a quart-size plastic bag. Seal the bag and have your youngster shake it until the color is thoroughly mixed. If too much coloring is added and the sand becomes wet, simply add more sand to absorb it. Have your toddler layer different colors of the sand into a jar for a keepsake. This is a great craft project for a playgroup.

Share and Tell

Everyone has heard of Show and Tell, but what about Share and Tell? Have each toddler bring something to playgroup that can be discussed as well as shared. (Put each item in a separate bag so toddlers can keep theirs a secret until it is their turn to share.) Sit in a circle and have the youngsters tell what they brought and why it is special, and then have them share with their friends. Ideas for items to share can include a favorite kind of candy (each child gets a piece), stickers (everyone gets to pick one), or a small trinket.

Silent Sleep

Have all the kids in the playgroup except for one lie on the ground in a sleeping position while you count to 10. Then have everyone remain quiet and motionless. The child who is still standing is "it" and will try to catch someone moving; if caught, that child is out and can now help watch the others for movement. No touching is allowed, although funny antics are encouraged. Whoever is the last to be out becomes "it" first the next time.

Slithering Snake

Have kids hold hands and appoint a leader who will act as the head of a snake. The leader will move around in a winding pattern with the other toddlers following in a line like a snake. Create some extra fun by having the leader weave through the line of arms of participants to create knots, which then must be untangled. If enough kids are participating, have the leader stand still and let others wrap like a coil. Unwind, and then have the leader go to the back and let the next child serve as the head of the snake.

Sock Hop

Crank up some fifties tunes and have a sock hop at your next playgroup get-together! Serve coke floats, have toddlers don fifties attire, and start a kid bop! (An inexpensive and easy look is rolled up jeans and either a pony tail or slicked back hair.)

Spin the Bottle

If kids in the playgroup can't decide or agree on what to do, come up with four or five options and place something that symbolizes each activity in a circle. (Activities can be reading a book, watching a movie, doing a craft, playing outside, etc.) Place a bottle in the center and spin it. Whatever the bottle points to when it stops will be the activity of the moment! Make sure that toddlers understand that whatever the bottle points to is what will be done first. This works well in a playgroup setting.

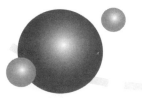

Spoon Races

A fun activity for toddlers is to have spoon races with friends. Place a grape, a piece of candy, or a small bouncy ball on a spoon and have kids balance the item as they run to a point and then race back! A plastic spoon is best in case a toddler slips and falls.

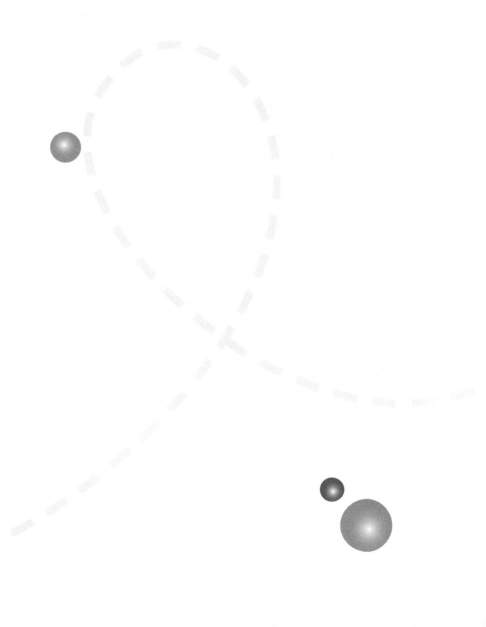

Treasure Jar

Create a treasure jar at your next playgroup. Kids are fascinated with shaking the bottle to uncover different items.

Materials

- baby food jars (the small size works great with toddler hands)
- sparkly or shiny items (beads, costume jewelry, or craft gemstones)
- glitter color of choice (metallic gold or silver with another color works well)
- light corn syrup
- warm water
- super glue or hot glue

Place the children's "treasures" in the jars. Sprinkle in some glitter and add corn syrup until the jars are about ¾ full. Next, fill them with warm water. Place lids on tightly and adults only should glue them closed. When the glue is set, let your toddlers shake their treasure and watch everything get mixed up. They'll be fascinated with how items settle and seem to float.

Veggie Pizza

Press crescent roll dough onto a pizza pan and bake according to the directions. Spread a light layer of ranch-style dressing or cream cheese with ranch dip mixed in. Let kids decorate their pizza with pieces of broccoli, carrots, celery, and any other veggie they'll eat. Cut into pizza slices and enjoy!

11

Smart Zone

With these great games, youngsters will have fun and learn at the same time!

Alphabet Book

Have your toddler create an alphabet book in an inexpensive notebook. Each page should feature items that start with the letter on that page. Toddlers like looking through magazines, so have them search through old issues for pictures to include in their book. Half the fun is cutting out the items and gluing them in, so toddler-safe scissors and a glue stick are strongly recommended. Once complete, this becomes a great "quiet time" book to look through!

Alphabet Weeks

Entertain your toddler and teach the alphabet at the same time by creating alphabet weeks. Each Sunday establish the letter of the week. Plan activities, food, and fun that begin with that letter. (For example, "B" week could include eating bread and blueberries, playing with building blocks, cleaning the basement, and wearing blue.) Find the letter on signs and in words in books. Either start in alphabetical order or let your toddler pick the letter of the week.

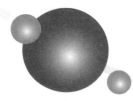

Back Track

A fun activity for younger toddlers is to take turns tracing shapes on each other's backs and then guessing what they are. Challenge older toddlers by tracing letters of the alphabet.

Balloon Science

Blow up a balloon and have your child rub it against her head to create some static electricity. Then have her see what it might stick to. The wall? The curtains? Her skin? Let your toddler observe what her hair (or yours) does when the balloon is held over it. Some crazy hairstyles can result!

Beginning, Middle, and End

Reading to your toddler will help him to recognize the beginning, middle, and end components of a book. Read books with very simple plots and quiz your toddler about what the characters are doing. Kids enjoy hearing the same stories over and over again, so during repeat readings invite your youngster to tell you what happens next and at the end of the story to encourage the building of narrative skills.

Bilingual Learning

The best time to teach a child a second language is when he's learning the first one. Expose your toddler to a second language and teach him about different cultures. Toddlers are learning to recognize speech patterns, and the earlier adults introduce a child to a second language, the easier it is discern its unique sounds. An easy way to do this is to create some simple flash cards with a picture in the middle, the English word above, and the second language word below. You'll be amazed at how quickly she progresses.

Body Outline Art

Trace a life-size, full-body outline of your child on paper. Then let your child draw in details, including clothing, fingernails, hair, and facial expression. For extra fun, give your child yarn to glue on for hair and even shoelaces! Cutouts can be glued on too (a cutout watch, shoes, hair bows, etc.).

Breakfast Blast

Leave a note under your toddler's plate or breakfast bowl each day (sticky notes work great for this). Start with simple symbols, such as a heart or a smiley face, and sign your name. As kids get older, write the first letter of an activity they will be doing that day and have them guess what it will be. (For example, write a letter "p" for park.) It's a fun way to encourage letter recognition and guessing!

Bug Match

Have your child help you draw bugs (ants, dragonflies, beetles, lady bugs, etc.) on construction paper. (You can also use pages from a coloring book or print outlines of bugs from the computer.) Then have her cut them out and color them, making sure that each bug is a different color but that the wings and both sides of individual insects match in color and other details. Cut the bugs in half lengthwise and place them in a box. Let your child take the bug halves out and match the pieces.

Character Chart

Create a chart of basic character traits that you'd like to instill in your child. Each week, talk about one trait and what it means in terms of his behavior. Start simply: Honesty, consideration, kindness, and effort are good starter words, and he should easily understand their meaning. You will not only expand your toddler's vocabulary; you will also teach values at the same time.

Color Magic

Buy an inexpensive tray of watercolor paints and let your toddler experiment with combining two or more colors to make a new one! Let your youngster create a unique new color and even name it! Paint a picture with all the new colors that were created.

Color Scavenger Hunt

Teach toddlers colors and their corresponding spellings with a color scavenger hunt! Mark recipe cards with basic colors (one per card) and write the name of each color beneath. Youngsters can then choose a card and hunt for items around them with the colors, and as skills progress, they can begin saying the letters that form the words of the colors. Be creative by using different shapes for the colors, so that green could be colored in a star-shape, red in a heart, blue in a diamond, and so forth. It's a good way to reinforce shapes too!

Creative Cookie Recipe

Ask your toddler to tell you the step-by-step process for baking chocolate chip cookies. Write down everything she says and keep it for a hilarious keepsake. This fun exercise also teaches kids sequencing.

Cup Stacking

Basic cup stacking is easy; it is also entertaining, educational, and inexpensive! Cup stacking is being used by more and more teachers to strengthen hand-eye coordination, encourage counting, and develop rhythm. While parents can certainly buy certain types of cups used for this particular activity, toddlers will equally benefit from inexpensive, medium-sized plastic cups bought at almost any store. Toddlers should start with stacking simple designs of three cups down, two on the next row above, and then one on top, and then expand their options from there. If you haven't seen cup stacking before, the general premise is to start with a stack of cups, quickly create a pyramid, and then restack the cups without having any topple over (speed and coordination are what count!). It's especially fun when done to music!

Egg Hunt Countdown

Add an educational spin to your next egg hunt by numbering the eggs from 1 to 12. Once all the eggs are found, have your toddler arrange the eggs in numerical order, 1–12. How high she orders them will depend on her age and ability, of course, so vary the game by numbering eggs up to where your child can count. This can be a fun hunt any time of year (not just at Easter). After she has counted, have your toddler hide the eggs for you to find!

Emoticon Flash Cards

Create some flash cards displaying blank emotion. Using the classic smiley-face style for simplicity, draw only the circle and the eyes. Have your toddler draw an expression on a face and then act out the emotion. You have to guess what it is. Then, switch! Start with simple emotions like happy, sad, mad, tired, surprised, and scared.

Expressions Flash Cards

Create some flash cards with facial expressions drawn on them. (Use simple smiley-face drawings.) Have your child choose a card and mimic the expression. It's up to you to guess which emotion your child is acting out— happy, sad, mad, surprised, confused, tired, or scared. This simple game encourages kids to think about feelings and to act out emotions.

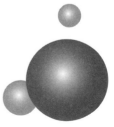

Eye Trick

Show your toddler how each eye can "look" at things differently. Extend your arms forward and place your hands together to form a small triangle. With both eyes open, look through the triangle and focus on an object. Next, close one eye. Does the item stay within the triangle? Switch to looking through the other eye. After your child has seen you demonstrate this activity, have him try it. While toddlers may not understand the dominant-eye concept, they'll like seeing how things seem to move when one of their eyes is closed.

Fetching Fun

Create some flash cards featuring simple pictures, shapes, or letters. These can easily be made using 3 by 5-inch index cards. Place three to five of them across the room. Describe a card and ask your toddler to retrieve it. Provide heaps of positive reinforcement each time your youngster gets the right card. Make this a regular game and increase the difficulty of the flash cards' contents as your toddler is able.

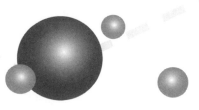

Flashlight Find

Tape index cards with shapes, colors, and simple words (your child's name, "dog," "bed," etc.) on the back of your child's door. As a before-bed activity, have your toddler turn off all lights in the room and use a flashlight to find items you name that appear on the door. Change the locations of the cards frequently so that the child begins to learn the actual shape or word rather than just memorizing its location on the door. Occasionally add a "surprise" index card that provides for something special (such as getting a favorite food for breakfast or renting a movie the next day).

Hot or Cold, Rain or Shine?

Inspire a budding meteorologist by having your toddler guess what the weather will be on a daily basis. Will today be hot? Cold? In-between? Is it going to rain or snow? Will it be sunny or cloudy? Using a small whiteboard, have your toddler draw a sun, raindrop, snowflake, or other weather symbol (with your help, as needed) to show her prediction. Older kids will enjoy tracking the actual temperature too.

Household Chores

One way to involve a youngster in the family routine is by having her help with chores. Give your toddler her own broom and dustpan or gardening gloves and trowel. Then encourage her to do such things as sweep the front porch or plant flowers, or let her help pull weeds while you are gardening. Youngsters think it is fun to help around the house, and you'll be teaching the important life lessons of responsibility and teamwork too!

International Greetings

Hola (OH-la)! Konichiwa (Koh-NEE-chee-wah)! Teach your child how to say hello in different languages, such as Spanish (hola) or Japanese (konichiwa). It's very easy to learn, and your child will delight in greeting others in a different language. There is a wealth of free information to provide you with pronunciations and different language listings on the Internet and at your local library.

M&M Alphabet Bingo

Here's a surefire way to get toddlers to practice their alphabet, learn a simple game, and get sweet rewards to boot! Mark several plain sheets of paper with a grid three rows down and three across. Place letters randomly in the 8 outside squares and leave the center square blank as a "free" space. (Make each sheet different. If your toddler is ready for a higher level, you can always make a more difficult bingo sheet.) Next, write all the letters you've written on the grid on a separate sheet of paper, cut each letter out so that it occupies its own separate square of paper, and then fold the squares and place them in a bowl. Explain to your toddler that the object of the game is to match three letters across, down, or diagonally. When a letter is drawn from the bowl, let your child see the letter and see if it is a match for anything on her sheet. If it is, she places an M&M on that letter (no eating them yet!). When a match of three connected letters is achieved, she gets to eat the M&Ms from that round! (Parents can always substitute a different treat, as preferred.) As your child's skills progress, don't let her view the letter drawn; instead, pronounce it and have her rely on her knowledge and memory of the letters. This simple game can also be done with numbers.

Man in the Moon

Can your toddler see a face in the moon? What does it look like? Does the face look different depending on the phases of the moon? Why or why not? Watch the moon together. Share information about the moon, its craters, and its phases to help foster an interest in space.

More or Less

Make a grab bag of simple items (marbles, pebbles, coins, etc.). Have your child reach in and grab some and then lay them out. Group the items and then count them together. Repeat the process until the bag is empty. Which group has the most and which have fewer? Which has the least?

Objects, Pictures, and Words

What's the difference between an object, a picture, and a word? Start this activity with common items, such as a pair of shoes, a picture of shoes, and the word *shoes* written on an index card. Have your youngster assess which is which and explain the differences as well as he can. Build on this concept by writing your child's name, having a photo of him, and having him look in the mirror at his actual self! This is a good early-learning concept for toddlers.

Opposite Day

Play a game of opposites. If you say "happy," she says "sad." You say "up," and she says "down." After three turns, reverse who says the initial word. This is a great travel game.

Paper Airplane Contest

It's amazing what you can create with a single sheet of paper, isn't it? Show your child how to make a paper airplane and have him make one too. Have an "air show" to see which plane flies the highest, farthest, fastest, and does the best loop-de-loops. Minimize any competition by allowing your toddler to switch aircraft, if desired, for each contest.

Paw Print Match

What type of animal track would a giraffe make? A bear? How about a bird? Create some cards that a toddler can use to match an animal with its tracks. Use pictures from a magazine or the Internet for animal identification and then draw basic tracks (visit a variety of Web sites for reference). Let your youngster match the animal photos to the appropriate tracks.

Phone Number Song

Experts encourage parents to teach kids their home phone numbers at an early age. This is achievable for kids as young as 3, so make it fun and practice, practice, practice! The child's song "Are You Sleeping?" ("Frère Jacques") works well for this because of its simple sing-song-and-repeat melody. Just think of the tune in your head and insert numbers in place of the lyrics. Sing it and then have your toddler sing it back to you. She'll have the number memorized in no time.

Plate Connection

At your next indoor play date, try the plate connection game for some brain-bending fun. Cut paper plates in half using different cuts (zigzag, rounded, jagged, etc.). Give each child a plate half and then have them walk around to their peers and try to match plate halves. Be sure to stress that the halves need to be a perfect fit to count as a match. When match buddies are found, have them sit down until all matches are located. This activity helps to build analytical thinking skills.

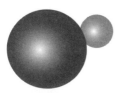

Raisin Magic

The next time you buy seedless grapes, set a few aside for an experiment. Place the grapes (washed and de-stemmed) on a paper plate. Cover the grapes with a kitchen towel or cheesecloth and place them in direct sunlight. Set aside a time each day to observe how they are changing, and consider making a raisin log (youngsters can draw what the grapes look like on the first day and after each viewing). Within 5–7 days the grapes will turn into raisins. Ask your child what happened. Where is the juice that was in the grape? Kids will be fascinated by the transformation.

Read and Repeat

One of the most effective and fun ways to teach early reading skills is through the "read and repeat" method. Let your child choose a favorite book. Then make reading it a game. You read a sentence and then have your toddler repeat it back. Heap on lots of praise! You'll be surprised by how quickly a toddler can memorize a simple story and then "read" it to others!

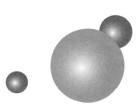

Shoe Math

Have your toddler collect one pair of shoes from each member of the family and sort them from largest to smallest. Ask which ones are widest, tallest, heaviest, and so on.

Skip Together

There's something about skipping together that transforms adults into school-aged kids once again. Most toddlers have to spend some time learning how to skip; it's a coordination skill that typically takes some practice to accomplish. Skip together down the sidewalk or even in a store for some laughs. Holding hands can add some extra charm!

Sound Game

Tell your toddler you're thinking of a sound and then sound it out. Can your child think of a word that begins with that sound? Can she identify the letter? This is a great game to play in the car or when waiting in the doctor's office or at the airport, and it helps foster listening skills.

Straw Measurements

Cut a number of plastic straws into different lengths. Have your toddler practice putting them in a line from shortest to tallest. After that, count the number of straws. How many are left if you take one straw away? Two? This is a good approach for teaching the concepts of bigger and smaller as well as simple math.

Touchy-feely Box

Use an empty tissue box to create a touchy-feely box. Secretly place different items in the box (only one item in the box at a time) and have your toddler reach inside to touch it and guess what it is. Alternate sizes and textures.

Trading Cards

One way to encourage kids to read is by having them earn trading cards on books they've finished. After your child reads a book, write the name of the book on a card (use index cards or something similar) and have your youngster decorate it. Display it prominently and proudly to show a growing collection. If possible, have same-age friends participate and let them swap books to increase their collections even more!

Vocabulary Building

Reading to your toddler will increase the number of words she is familiar with. As you read, stop when you get to a word your youngster may not know. Explain the word and encourage her to say it. At the end of the book, go back to those new words and see if she remembers their meanings and pronunciations.

Water and Ice

Demonstrate that water can be either solid or liquid by having your child participate in a simple experiment. Drink some water together while talking about places where water comes from (such as a river, lake, or rain). Have your child fill a small container of water and place it in the freezer. When the water is frozen, take it out of the freezer and talk to your toddler about the ways water can be solid (snow and ice cubes, for example). Leave the container out on the counter. What begins to happen?

Weekly Countdown

Help your toddler learn the notion of 7-day weeks by stringing 7 beads on a rope or string and hanging it horizontally in his room. Start all the beads at one end and each morning have your youngster slide 1 bead over to represent the day of the week until all the beads are at the other end. On Saturday night, before bedtime, have your child slide all the beads back over to the starting place.

What's in the Box?

Place something in a box and let your toddler try to guess what it is by giving him clues. Keep it simple to avoid frustration. For example, "I have something that is long and skinny. It has a point at one end and an eraser at the other. It is used to write with. What's in the box?" A pencil, of course!

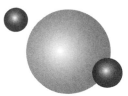

12

The Sickies

What can parents do with kids who are too sick for daycare or leaving the house but not so ill that they are bed-bound? These activities to do with sick kids will keep them calm and well rested while they recover.

Bath Time Adventure

Sometimes getting kids who don't feel well to take a leisurely bath can be a challenge, but not when they get to make their bathtub entertainment!

Materials
- foam paper or other foam material (including inexpensive kitchen sponges)
- scissors (toddler-safe)

There is no need to rely on precut commercial shapes for bath time fun. Let your less-than-healthy youngster pick a theme and with a few snips and some imagination, bath time can be fun and not a chore. Maybe your toddler wants a flower garden (simple flower shapes in multiple colors) or to be a pirate (black eye patch, treasure chest, or sword). Once your child has picked a special theme, you and he can cut away!

Bedside Picnic

When your child is under the weather but you need him to eat, pull out a blanket, get out your picnic gear, and serve a meal picnic-style. It even makes comfort foods like good old chicken noodle soup taste better!

Boo-boo Bunnies

Create these simple boo-boo bunnies and give them to your sick toddler or to others when they're down and out or have a boo-boo.

Materials
- small towel or washcloth (you pick the color)
- rubber band (or use clear plastic ponytail holders)
- thin ribbon
- google eyes
- small pom-pom (for the nose)
- craft glue

Fold the washcloth in half to form a triangle, then roll it from the top point to the long side and fold in half. Fold washcloth in half again so that the loose ends point back toward the original fold. Place a rubber band around the washcloth about 2 inches from the fold. Cover the rubber band with ribbon and make a bow. Glue the eyes and pom-pom nose onto the bunny. When the glue is dry, either insert a small ice pack or small plastic bag (snack size) inside the bunny's tummy section, with instructions to add ice to the bag, or place a frozen ice pack inside the boo-boo bunny and give to toddlers to relieve ouchies.

Celery Transformation

Fill two clear glasses with water and add a different color of food coloring to each one (use several drops). Slit a celery stalk from the bottom to a fourth of the way from the top. Put a stalk in each glass, cut side down. Watch what begins to happen over the course of a few hours and talk with your child about the changes. What color do the stalks begin to turn? What happens to the top part (where the celery is not split)? Remove the celery from the water, cut it, then let your toddler look inside.

Cheer Chants

Lift your child's spirits by creating some simple cheers together to help boost spirits and recovery (nothing strenuous, obviously). Write them down for future use. Who knows? Your toddler may need to be the one to cheer you up when you're under the weather at a later date.

Colorful Carnations

Let your toddler create a bouquet of custom get-well flowers for himself. Place a carnation stem under running water and cut about 1 inch off the bottom. Put food dye of any color in a vase with warm water and place the carnation in the vase. Your toddler will marvel at how the carnation "drinks up" the colored water and changes colors.

Cotton Ball Clouds

Toddlers will love creating big, fluffy clouds on a blue sky with this simple craft. Afterward, if weather permits and your toddler is homebound but not very ill (such as recovering from pinkeye or a cold), take her outdoors to marvel at the clouds in the sky. (Sicker toddlers can also look at the sky through a window.)

Materials
- blue construction paper
- glue stick
- white cotton balls
- glitter (if available)

Have your child draw cloud shapes on paper using a glue stick and then create clouds by gluing on cotton balls. (Have them tear the cotton balls apart a little to create more realistic cloud shapes). For something extra-special, add a little glitter (sunbeams, of course!).

Counting All Nurses!

If your child is at the hospital or doctor's office, see how many nurses (or other medical practitioners) she can spot over a certain time period. Have a contest to see who spots more.

Fairy Catcher

What better time to believe in fairies than when we're young? Have your toddler create a magic fairy bag for catching fairies. Supply her with a flashlight so she can spot a fairy while resting. If she catches a fairy, she gets to make a special wish! When your child isn't watching, sprinkle some magical fairy dust into the bag, or perhaps an occasional treat or note, for extra excitement!

Fish Faces

Show your toddler how to make fish faces. Suck in your cheeks, bug out your eyes, and make your lips all goofy! Try different types of silly fish looks, and don't forget to add your hands for gills or fins. A few minutes of this promises to cheer up any guppy!

Food Art

Have fun with your youngster's favorite food. Create a fun face by making an open-face peanut butter sandwich. Use a banana slice for the nose, grapes for eyes, cranberries for the mouth, and grape jelly for the hair! Use whatever foods your toddler likes and let her be creative! The best part? She'll love eating her artistic creation even when she may not have the best appetite!

Freaky Hair Fun

Just think of the fun that a little hair gel, clips, and pony-tail holders can bring to a housebound toddler. Start by making crazy styles with your child's hair; then it's your turn! This is a sure way to take the focus off a minor illness. Capture the moment with a photo as a keepsake.

Fruit Smoothie

Make a healthy snack more fun by showing kids how to make a fruit smoothie with yogurt and fresh fruit. Depending on personal preference, you can add in some milk, ice, or ice cream. Make it special by serving it in a fancy glass!

Get-well Bookmark

Have your child create a personalized get-well bookmark using paper, felt, foam, and decorations. If your toddler is in the hospital and feels up to it, bring supplies for her to give out to other kids on the floor to cheer them up too.

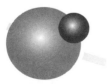

Handmade Get-well Cards

Having your sick child create get-well cards for others who may be in worse shape is a great way to help him feel better and take his mind off his own illness. If your toddler is home with a short-term illness and recovery is in the near future, have him create some get-well cards for others who may be sick. Youngsters are quick to empathize with the feelings and well-being of other kids.

Hat's On!

Hats can brighten a case of the sickies, so keep an accessible collection of hats that your toddler can don any time. Show your youngster how you can change or update a hat by flipping the brim, adding a flower, or wearing it differently.

Homemade Goo

If your child is well enough to get out of bed and enjoy some quiet play, consider making some homemade goo to help drive boredom away.

Ingredients (mix in no particular order)
- 1 cup flour
- ¼ cup salt
- 2 tablespoons of cream of tartar
- 1 tablespoon cooking oil
- 1 cup water
- food coloring (optional and as desired)

You probably already have all the ingredients in your pantry, and this is something you and your toddler can make—and play with—together! Keep it in an airtight container or resealable bag. Dispose of it after a few days (you can always make more!).

Jell-O for One

Jell-O is often on a doctor's approved-foods list when a toddler is sick. If your child is up to it, have him help you make some Jell-O for snacks. It's quick, easy, and easy on the stomach. Mix up your child's favorite gelatin flavor according to the recipe and pour it into plastic ice-cube trays to set for single-serving convenience.

Love Sandwich

Show your toddler how much you love him by making a "love sandwich." After making his favorite sandwich, cut the bread into a heart shape before serving it.

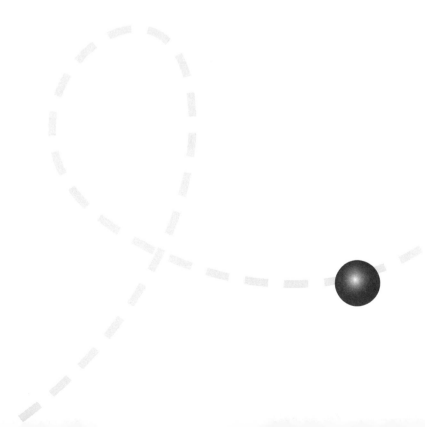

Make Your Own Bubbles

Where are bubbles when you need them most? Here's a simple bubble recipe that will help cheer up an under-the-weather toddler.

Materials
- 1 cup liquid dish detergent or nonirritating baby shampoo
- 3 cups water

Simply mix the materials and pour into cups; then blow bubbles with straws, bubble pipes, or wands that you can make yourself with thin wire. Curious toddlers can usually find kitchen items that work well for bubble creations.

Medicine Countdown

If your toddler has to take medicine to overcome an ailment, start a countdown to track how many doses are required. Mark the days on a sheet of paper and, if desired, divide each day into doses too. Let your toddler choose a sticker or stamp to mark each successful dose taken!

Object Find

If your child is hospitalized, help alleviate his anxiety over being in a strange environment by creating an object-find game. Have your toddler look for certain objects commonly found in a hospital room, such as a clock, sink, television, controls for the bed, toilet, nurses station, and call button.

Paint Roller Bath

Give your toddler a new, small, foam paint roller and plastic paint liner. Use shaving cream, bubble bath, or liquid soap as paint, and let your sick toddler paint up the town while taking a bath or shower (under adult supervision). Your toddler will like rolling "paint" over his body or on top of bath toys, and the mess will literally rinse right away!

Pajama Day

Nothing feels quite as comfy as pj's, and having a slightly sick toddler gives everyone at home an excuse to declare a Pajama Day. Bring a favorite pillow, stuffed animals, and blanket or sleeping bag into the living room to create a "snuggle bed" area. Pop in a movie of your child's choosing and snack on cereal and other breakfast foods (no matter what time of day it is!). String some Cheerios or Froot Loops onto yarn, string, or pipe cleaners to make "cereal necklaces," and snack on them while watching a favorite show. (Toddlers love the notion of making "edible art.")

Sick Day Rituals

Create a "sick day ritual" that is performed whenever any member of the family becomes ill. The ritual could be serving the apple sauce (or food of choice) to the ill family member in a special chair, or maybe everyone in the family changes into pj's as soon as they get home from work or school in support of the sick member, or the sickie might choose what the family watches on TV during television time. Make it a ritual that everyone likes to practice, but be sure that it doesn't create cases of "wannabe sickies."

Sick Nurse

When a child is sick, sometimes it can help his spirits to nursemaid a beloved stuffed animal or doll back to health while recovering. Have your child take his buddy's temperature, give medicine, serve chicken noodle soup, and tuck the patient in for a nap.

Sickie Chaser

Your toddler can help to chase away a case of the sickies with this homemade noisemaker.

Materials
- 2 paper plates
- cotton balls
- markers, crayons, paint, glitter, or other household items, as desired, for decorating
- craft glue
- plastic whistle (whatever parents can handle)

Stuff cotton balls between two plates and glue shut. (As another option, you can also punch holes in the rims of the plates about an inch apart and lace the plates together using string or yarn.) Tie some yarn to the bottom of the plate and tie on a plastic whistle to "blow" away the sickies. (There are some inexpensive whistles that aren't too loud.) This craft doesn't take long, and kids who are not feeling their best will still enjoy this simple activity.

Sick-off

Help your child fend off the sick blues by having a "sickest looking face" contest. Make the most ill-looking, silliest faces you can at each other and just DARE each other not to smile!

Silly "Sick" Book

Staple pages of plain paper together and have your toddler create a silly sick book or journal. Your youngster can illustrate how she feels, what foods she is eating, things she is doing while recovering, and what she plans to do when she is well. Be sure to date it and hold onto it as a keepsake. This activity serves as a way for kids to think about their illness in a lighthearted way and look forward to their recovery!

Sponge Island

Tempt a not-feeling-so-well toddler into taking a soothing bath with this fun bathtub activity. Float some kitchen sponges bearing small toys (miniature cars, small dolls, or other items of interest to your child) around the island (your child). Create some waves and wet weather to set the toys in motion and to keep your toddler in the tub a little longer.

Wellness Book

Have your toddler create a "When I'm Well" book of thing she likes to do. It can be as simple as cutting photos of activities or favorite foods from magazines, gluing them onto half sheets of paper, stapled at the top, and drawing a picture on the cover. This activity helps kids have something to look forward to when they're better.

Wet Hands

Have your child wet a hand with very warm water (be careful that it's not too hot for your toddler!). Keep the other hand dry. Have him shake off the water and wave both his hands in the air. Ask him which hand feels cooler. Teach your toddler that as water evaporates into the air it carries away the heat and makes you feel cooler. That's the same concept our body uses when we sweat or have a fever.

Index by Activity Title

C

Q

R

About the Author

Robin McClure is a professional writer and a busy mom of three very active kids. She has served as the About.com Guide to Child Care since 2004 and has worked in the fields of public education and continuing education for 13 years. She lives in North Richland Hills, Texas.